URBAIN GRANDIER

Borgo Press Books Edited & Translated by FRANK J. MORLOCK

Anna Karenina: A Play in Five Acts, by Edmond Guiraud, from Leo Tolstoy
Anthony: A Play in Five Acts, by Alexandre Dumas, Père
The Children of Captain Grant: A Play in Five Acts, by Jules Verne and Adolphe d'Ennery
Crime and Punishment: A Play in Three Acts, by Frank J. Morlock, from Fyodor Dostoyevsky
Don Quixote: A Play in Three Acts, by Victorien Sardou, from Miguel de Cervantes
The Dream of a Summer Night: A Fantasy Play in Three Acts, by Paul Meurice
Falstaff: A Play in Four Acts, by William Shakespeare, John Dennis, William Kendrick, and Frank J. Morlock
The Idiot: A Play in Three Acts, by Frank J. Morlock, from Fyodor Dostoyevsky
Jesus of Nazareth: A Play in Three Acts, by Paul Demasy
The Jew of Venice: A Play in Five Acts, by Ferdinand Dugué
Joan of Arc: A Play in Five Acts, by Charles Desnoyer
The Lily of the Valley: A Play in Five Acts, by Théodore Barrière and Arthur de Beauplan, from Honoré de Balzac
Lord Byron in Venice: A Play in Three Acts, by Jacques Ancelot
Louis XIV and the Affair of the Poisons: A Play in Five Acts, by Victorien Sardou
The Man Who Saw the Devil: A Play in Two Acts, by Gaston Leroux
Mathias Sandorf: A Play in Three Acts, by Jules Verne and William Busnach
Michael Strogoff: A Play in Five Acts, by Jules Verne and Adolphe d'Ennery
Les Misérables: A Play in Two Acts, by Victor Hugo, Paul Meurice, and Charles Victor Hugo
The Mysteries of Paris: A Play in Five Acts, by Eugène Sue and Prosper Dinaux
Ninety-Three: A Play in Four Acts, by Victor Hugo and Paul Meurice
Notes from the Underground: A Play in Two Acts, by Frank J. Morlock, from Fyodor Dostoyevsky
Outrageous Women: Lady MacBeth and Other French Plays, edited by Frank J. Morlock
Peau de Chagrin: A Play in Five Acts, by Louis Judicis, from Honoré de Balzac
A Raw Youth: A Play in Five Acts, by Frank J. Morlock, from Fyodor Dostoyevsky
Richard Darlington: A Play in Three Acts, by Alexandre Dumas, Père
The San Felice: A Play in Five Acts, by Maurice Drack, from Alexander Dumas, Père
Saul and David: A Play in Five Acts, by Voltaire
Shylock, the Merchant of Venice: A Play in Three Acts, by Alfred de Vigny
Socrates: A Play in Three Acts, by Voltaire
The Stendhal Hamlet Scenarios and Other Shakespearean Shorts from the French, edited by Frank J. Morlock
A Summer Night's Dream: A Play in Three Acts, by Joseph-Bernard Rosier and Adolphe de Leuwen
Urbain Grandier and the Devils of Loudon: A Play in Four Acts, by Alexandre Dumas, Père
The Voyage Through the Impossible: A Play in Three Acts, by Jules Verne and Adolphe d'Ennery
The Whites and the Blues: A Play in Five Acts, by Alexandre Dumas, Père
William Shakespeare: A Play in Six Acts, by Ferdinand Dugué

URBAIN GRANDIER AND THE DEVILS OF LOUDON

A Play in Four Acts

by

Alexandre Dumas, Père

Translated and Adapted by Frank J. Morlock

The Borgo Press

An Imprint of Wildside Press LLC

MMX

Copyright © 2000, 2010 by Frank J. Morlock

All rights reserved. No part of this book may be reproduced without the expressed written consent of the author. Professionals are warned that this material, being fully protected under the copyright laws of the United States of America, and all other countries of the Berne and Universal Copyright Convention, is subject to a royalty. All rights, including all forms of performance now existing or later invented, but not limited to professional, amateur, recording, motion picture, recitation, public reading, radio, television broadcasting, DVD, and Role Playing Games, and all rights of translation into foreign languages, are expressly reserved. Particular emphasis is placed on the question of readings, and all uses of these plays by educational institutions, permission for which must be secured in advance from the author's publisher, Wildside Press, 9710 Traville Gateway Dr. #234, Rockville, MD 20850 (phone 301-762-1305).

www.wildsidebooks.com

FIRST WILDSIDE EDITION

CONTENTS

Cast of Characters 7

Prologue, Scene 1 9
Prologue, Scene 2 44
Prologue, Scene 3 70
Act I, Scene 4 73
Act I, Scene 5 93
Act I, Scene 6 108
Act I, Scene 7 120
Act II, Scene 8 121
Act II, Scene 9 139
Act III, Scene 10 166
Act III, Scene 11 176
Act IV, Scene 12 204
Act IV, Scene 13 213

About the Editor 222

DEDICATION

To

CONRAD CADY

For His Unwavering Support of My Translations of Dumas

CAST OF CHARACTERS

Urbain Grandier
The Cardinal-Duke de Richelieu
Maurizio
Olivier de Sourdis
Laubardemont
L'Abbé Grillau
The Bailiff
Mignon
Marshal de Schomberg
Nogaret
Barace
A Priest
A Police Officer (aka an Exempt)
A Clerk of Court
Two Men of the People
A Monk
Two Servants
Two Sentinels
A Jailor
A Swiss Guard
A Postilion
Daniel (played by a female)
Jeanne de Laubardemont
Ursula de Sable
The Countess

Madame Grandier
Bianca
Women of the People.

PROLOGUE

Scene 1

A large terrace with arcades surmounted by a gallery extending the length of the stage. To the left, a pavilion with a usable balcony. To the right, an entrance with a stairway of eight or ten steps going up to a higher floor. One gets to the terrace by a large stairway parallel to the other one which leans against the pavilion on the left. Through the arcades can be seen the city of Casal—then the plain and above the plain, the snowy chain of the Alps.

A sentinel at the foot of the stairway; three or four house servants grouped on the terrace.

1ST SERVANT

It's him.

2ND SERVANT

Why no—since he's in Mantua. How can you think it's he?

1ST SERVANT

Well, he's back from Mantua—because he left Casal, do you think he'll never return?

WOMAN

I'm of Bartholomew's opinion. I think it's he.

1ST SERVANT

It's indeed he—since he's riding the same horse which he had when he left three months ago.

WOMAN

Ah! Now, I recognize him. The Countess will be overjoyed.

1ST SERVANT

It's Miss Bianca who will be sad.

2ND SERVANT

Sad to see her brother?

1ST SERVANT

Shut up—a man who makes a woman enter a convent when she'd prefer to marry—is that what you call a brother?

WOMAN

Oh! I want to be first to announce this good news to the Countess.

1ST SERVANT

She's coming—pay your court.

WOMAN

What are you doing?—it's not your expense.

(calling)

Countess—Madam Countess.

(The Countess at the top of the stairs. Then Maurizio coming up the stairs while his mother comes down.)

COUNTESS

My son?

WOMAN

Himself! Here—he's coming up the stairs.

(The servants salute.)

COUNTESS

Is it you, my dear child?

MAURIZIO

Yes, mother.

(to servants)

That's fine, good day.

COUNTESS

Where are you coming from that you come to us without warning?

MAURIZIO

Because until a week ago, I was still unaware that I must come. His Highness, the Grand Duke, having learned that the French, led by the Cardinal, were marching on Casal, sent me to bring the news. My word, I didn't waste my time and I've come just in time to assist in the taking of the city. It is the most beautiful pearl in his Ducal crown, which he had lost and which he's just recovered. Whoever tells him first won't be badly received and I hope it will be me.

COUNTESS

So Casal's surrendered?

MAURIZIO

Yes—the news is quite fresh and I saw the governor in person bring the keys to the Cardinal—about a quarter of an hour ago.

COUNTESS

Would you have recognized a prince of the church in the costume His Eminence is wearing?

MAURIZIO

No, mother, but I recognize the Conqueror of Rochelle, of Pas de Suze, Privas, the First Minister of King Louis XIII even. As for the rest, assuredly this costume is more useful to him than the cloak of a cardinal.

In the job he's doing, a helmet is better than a fancy pin. Is it true that yesterday a Spanish bullet had the insolence to flatten itself on his Cuirass? I heard that repeated in the camp? They even added that, without a soldier from the regiment of Poitou who rescued Milord from an ambush His Eminence would have been the prisoner of the governor of Casal—rather than the governor of Casal being the prisoner of His Eminence.

COUNTESS

In fact, there's been talk of nothing else all night—they've looked for the soldier but without result.

MAURIZIO

The Devil—there's someone who can be praised for his modesty—but I'm not concerned—he will be found.

COUNTESS

You are so well informed in all things that I won't ask you if you know that the Cardinal-Duke is doing us the honor of choosing this palace for his hotel.

MAURIZIO

And it's an honor that should have cost us our palace, if things had not turned out so. In any case, I presume that my good mother has not let the opportunity escape to speak to him of her son's vocation for diplomacy and her daughter's for the cloister.

COUNTESS

Yes, Maurizio, yes—I have spoken to him about you—and he's promised me to recommend you to the Duke of Mantua.

MAURIZIO

And what did he say about my sister?

COUNTESS

He understands that a great fortune is necessary to the heir to a great name while such a fortune is of no use to a young girl who is not called upon to play a great role in the world.

MAURIZIO

And you have obtained?

COUNTESS

A dispensation for Bianca. Tomorrow she will enter convent—and in a month, she will make her profession.

MAURIZIO

And has he seen her?

COUNTESS

Bianca? No.

MAURIZIO

And where is she?

COUNTESS

In the pavilion.

MAURIZIO

This pavilion is very isolated, mother.

COUNTESS

I have the key to the door and the jalousie. No one can go down to the terrace except by this stairway that a watchman guards night and day—and after the Ave Maria is sounded, no one can leave the house without an order or passport from the Cardinal.

MAURIZIO

Then I see you have foreseen everything—oh—oh—what's that?

COUNTESS

The Cardinal is returning doubtless.

COUNTESS

It is he! See, Madam, what a warrior-like shape he has on horseback—wouldn't you say he's a consummate knight? Sound the trumpets and wave the flags.

(They obey on the gallery. Fanfare.)

(Three men enter to relieve the sentinel on the stairway.)

NEW SENTINEL

The password?

SENTINEL

(standing down)

Paris and Piedmont.

NEW SENTINEL

That's fine.

WOMAN

Countess?

COUNTESS

What is it?

WOMAN

A French lady who reeks of nobility asks permission from the Countess to await the Cardinal on the terrace. She has a request to present to the Cardinal.

COUNTESS

Have her up.

WOMAN

Come, Madam.

(A veiled lady passes before the sentinel who looks at her attentively through her veil, she salutes the Countess and goes to lean against one of the arcades. Servants come down the stairway, entering by the side door, and group around the terrace and the gallery. Some trumpets proceed the Cardinal. Men and instruments bear French arms. Then come the banners of the Cardinal on the same rung with the Banners of France. Then an officer appears bearing the keys to Casal, followed by the Cardinal, in armor, sword at his side; a page bears his helmet, it has a red skull cap, then comes Marshal Schomberg, the Marshal of the force, the Marshal of Marilhac, Olivier de Sourdis, Barace, Nogaret, and other gentleman and captains.)

SCHOMBERG

His Eminence wishes to see the soldier that yesterday came to his aid.

CARDINAL

Say—who saved my life—Marshal. Where is he?

SCHOMBERG

He's the one presenting arms to Your Excellency.

CARDINAL

Ah, ah, in fact—I recognize him.

(to sentinel)

What's your name, sir?

SENTINEL

Urbain Grandier, Milord.

CARDINAL

Where were you born?

GRANDIER

In the town of Rovère, near Sable, in Lower Maine.

CARDINAL

What regiment do you belong to?

GRANDIER

The Regiment of Poitou.

CARDINAL

How long have you been a soldier?

GRANDIER

For three years.

CARDINAL

Is this the first time you've been under my orders?

GRANDIER

I was at the siege of La Rochelle, at the attack on Pas de Suze, at the taking of Privas.

CARDINAL

Why is it you are not yet an officer, being so brave?

GRANDIER

To be an officer, Milord, it's not enough to be brave, one must also be noble.

CARDINAL

And you are not?

GRANDIER

I've told the Marshal, I am a poor peasant.

CARDINAL

Can you read?

GRANDIER

(smiling)

Yes, Milord.

CARDINAL

Why are you smiling?

GRANDIER

I was wrong. Pride is one of the seven deadly sins.

CARDINAL

(turning to Schomberg)

What's he say, Marshal—

SCHOMBERG

He said, Milord, or rather he didn't say, but I am going to say it for him.

GRANDIER

Milord Marshal.

SCHOMBERG

Come on! No false, or rather stupid modesty, Grandier. Perhaps you'll never have a chance like this again. What this honest lad didn't tell you, Milord, is that being the nephew of a very wise man, named Claude Grandier, he studied astrology and alchemy under his uncle—that having been raised at the Jesuit College of Bordeaux, he learned ancient languages so that he speaks Latin like Mathurin Regnier, and Greek like Conrad—all that without counting English and German—moreover, he's a painter, musician, mathematician—what do I know?

CARDINAL

Oh! Oh! That's plenty of learning for one man.

(to Grandier)

Who is your Captain, my friend?

GRANDIER

Mr. Olivier de Sourdis.

CARDINAL

Nephew of Mr. d'Escoubleau de Sourdis, Archbishop of Bordeaux?

SCHOMBERG

Himself.

CARDINAL

Mr. Olivier de Sourdis is here?

OLIVIER

(coming forward)

Here I am, Milord.

CARDINAL

You know this man, Mr. de Sourdis?

OLIVIER

Yes, sir.

CARDINAL

For how long?

OLIVIER

As long as I've known myself.

CARDINAL

Are you from the same province?

OLIVIE

I am from La Flèche, Milord and we went to college together. I recruited him.

CARDINAL

What are you talking about?

OLIVIER

At college, he was the best of students. In the army he's one of our best soldiers.

CARDINAL

And is he as learned as they say?

OLIVIER

More, probably, Milord.

CARDINAL

Why, being so learned was he made a soldier instead of a clerk?

OLIVIER

(approaching the Cardinal)

I think the poor lad is in love with a daughter of the nobility, Milord, and he had hopes of making his way by the sword.

CARDINAL

Then he's a man that can be promoted.

OLIVIER

That would be just.

CARDINAL

You will answer to me for him.

OLIVIER

As for myself, Milord.

CARDINAL

That's fine—

(turning to a man in black who has taken notes)

You heard?

SECRETARY

You will hear from me, Grandier.

GRANDIER

I will humbly await the orders of Your Eminence.

(Olivier and the Secretary are three paces in the rear. In turning the Cardinal finds himself face to face with the Countess and Maurizio.)

CARDINAL

Oh, it's you, our gracious hostess?

COUNTESS

Does His Eminence permit me to present my son—Count Maurizio dei Albizzio?

CARDINAL

You've already spoken to me of this young man, it seems to me?

COUNTESS

Yes, Milord and even His Eminence has deigned to promise me his high protection.

CARDINAL

You ardently love your son, Countess?

COUNTESS

Ardently, yes, Milord.

CARDINAL

You love him to the point of sacrificing his sister Bianca for him?

COUNTESS

To the point of sacrificing my life to him.

CARDINAL

You belong to Duke of Mantua, Count?

MAURIZIO

I am his private secretary, Milord.

CARDINAL

He sent you to Piedmont?

MAURIZIO

For news of Casal, yes, Milord.

CARDINAL

You wish to return to him with a powerful recommendation.

MAURIZIO

I should look on myself as a happy man if I had that of Your Eminence.

CARDINAL

Take the keys of the city I have just reconquered for him—and take them to him on my behalf. That is, I think, the best recommendation I can give you.

MAURIZIO

Oh—Milord!

CARDINAL

That's not all. Listen here carefully. I want to have, from time to time, news of His Highness, who I love and greatly esteem. The interest I bear him is so great that I am indifferent to nothing which may happen to him, nothing which he does, nothing which he even thinks. I authorize you to write me directly, once a week, Count Maurizio.

MAURIZIO

Milord!

CARDINAL

Go, sir, your fortune is in your own hands from this moment.

OLIVIER

(who has heard)

Oh, poor Bianca—that explains to me why he's condemned you.

MAURIZIO

(embracing the Countess)

Goodbye, mother, goodbye.

(low)

I commend my sister to you.

(Maurizio leaves.)

THE VEILED WOMAN

(advancing towards the Cardinal kneeling)

Milord.

CARDINAL

Who are you?

THE VEILED WOMAN

I am the daughter of one of your most devoted servants.

CARDINAL

What do you wish?

THE VEILED WOMAN

For Your Eminence to hear my confession.

CARDINAL

Why come to me, instead of all others?

THE VEILED WOMAN

Because my crime is so great that you alone, Milord, in virtue of the powers you hold at Rome, are great enough to absolve me.

CARDINAL

Follow me.

(The Cardinal leaves—everyone follows him except Grandier, Olivier, Nogaret and Barace.)

OLIVIER

Nogaret! Barace.

NOGARET AND BARACE

We are here.

OLIVIER

You have told me that I could count on you?

NOGARET

And we repeat it.

OLIVIER

Good. Barace, go wait for me on the route to Cérisoles.

BARACE

With how many horses?

OLIVIER

With three, one for her—one for me and one for my lackey.

BARACE

We are not to accompany you?

OLIVIER

I am making you run enough danger.

NOGARET

And what must I do?

OLIVIER

Go, find the silken ladder; assure yourself of its strength, and come rejoin me here.

BARACE

So—I am to be down there with the horses.

OLIVIER

All saddled—all bridled.

NOGARET

And I here, with the ladder.

NOGARET AND BARACE

But the watchman.

OLIVIER

It's Grandier—I know him—I am going to make him privy to my affair.

NOGARET AND BARACE

Fine.

OLIVIER

Go.

(The two young men leave.)

OLIVIER

(going to Grandier)

Urbain.

GRANDIER

My Captain.

OLIVIER

We are old friends, right?

GRANDIER

You mean, you've done me the honor of being friendly to me for a long while?

OLIVIER

You've sometimes spoken to me of your gratitude for the little services I've had the opportunity to render you.

GRANDIER

Ten times I've told you the day that you ask me for my life, my life will be yours.

OLIVIER

Well, if you think you owe me something, the time has come to acquit yourself towards me, and even more.

GRANDIER

I am listening.

OLIVIER

Grandier, you hold my joy, my happiness in your hands.

GRANDIER

Tell me what to do, sir.

OLIVIER

Listen Grandier, I'm in love. You know what it is to be in love? Well, I love Bianca the way you love Ursula.

GRANDIER

Then you love greatly and righteously, my Captain.

OLIVIER

If they were kidnapping Ursula what would you do?

GRANDIER

I would kill whoever took her from me.

OLIVIER

Yes—but if you could not kill him? If the one who took her from you was her brother.

GRANDIER

Her brother?

OLIVIER

And if they kidnapped her to give her to God despite herself?

GRANDIER

They are taking her from you by making her a nun?

OLIVIER

Yes.

GRANDIER

They are giving her to God, despite herself—and she has a mother.

OLIVIER

Oh! It's this mother who is without pity, without bowels—it's the mother who sacrifices her fortune to her son.

GRANDIER

Why don't you address yourself to the Cardinal, who has friendship for you, sir?

OLIVIER

Because the Cardinal's interests pass before his friendship—because he had purchased the soul of the brother by promising him his sister will be a nun, because he needs a spy near the Duke of Mantua, and Maurizio dei Albizzio will be that spy—on the condition they bury his sister alive—his sister who, possesses the entire fortune being the child of the Count's first wife.

GRANDIER

And when will they take her to convent.

OLIVIER

Tomorrow.

GRANDIER

Does she love you, sir?

OLIVIER

As I love her, Urbain.

GRANDIER

So that she's determined to flee.

OLIVIER

She's only waiting for the signal.

GRANDIER

You must carry her off then.

OLIVIER

Oh—my friend—you will help me then?

GRANDIER

Have I not told you that my life was yours? After my guard, dispose of me, sir.

OLIVIER

No, no—you don't need to leave your post—on the contrary.

GRANDIER

How's that?

OLIVIER

She's there, in this pavilion, locked in her room, but I have the key to the jalousie which I had made from a wax imprint she tossed to me.

GRANDIER

(becoming serious)

Then, hurry to take her before the Ave Maria, my Captain.

OLIVIER

Before the Ave Maria?

GRANDIER

Yes.

OLIVIER

Impossible! The Ave Maria is going to sound in ten minutes.

GRANDIER

Because after the Ave it will be more impossible still, sir.

OLIVIER

I don't understand. Explain yourself.

GRANDIER

She must come down from that window, right?

OLIVIER

Yes.

GRANDIER

She must leave by this stairway?

OLIVIER

Yes.

GRANDIER

Well, my Captain, after the last tone of the Ave Maria, no one can leave the castle without an order or passport from the Cardinal—it's the order.

OLIVIER

But sure you are on guard until nine o'clock.

GRANDIER

(sadly)

Yes, my Captain, and it is precisely because it's I who am on guard that you cannot pass.

OLIVIER

Grandier?

GRANDIER

The order, my Captain.

OLIVIER

Grandier, your memory is very short and your devotion very scrupulous.

GRANDIER

You are an officer, sir—and consequently, you know what an order is. Sir, pardon me.

OLIVIER

Well, as your officer, I order you to let me pass—you hear?

GRANDIER

My Captain, I offered you my life. Kill me, I won't give the alarm, I won't cry out "Who goes there". I won't defend myself—I advise you to kill me, for on my honor—living, no—I will not let you pass.

OLIVIER

Oh! My God! My God! When everything is ready, when I can touch happiness—when it is here—! Grandier, in the name of heaven—look, look, the Ave Maria is ringing.

GRANDIER

Be careful, someone is coming.

OLIVIER

What to do, my God, what to do?

GRANDIER

It's a woman—her mother perhaps—go away.

OLIVIER

(rushing down the step)

Oh! Grandier, Grandier! Won't you let yourself be softened.

(The Ave Maria rings slowly during the remainder of the scene. The veiled woman waits until Olivier goes off—then she approaches Grandier and raises her veil.)

GRANDIER

(recoiling)

Jeanne de Laubardemont.

JEANNE

Ah, you recognized me, Grandier? That's a good omen.

GRANDIER

What do you want from me, Madam? And what are you doing in Italy?

JEANNE

I want to remind you that you loved me, Grandier—and I've come to tell you that I still love you.

GRANDIER

Alas, Madam, that love of which you speak was the first love of my youth—my youth has stolen away and taken its dreams along with it.

JEANNE

Grandier, since you left Bordeaux, and it's been more than five years since I lost sight of you, I've been convinced of one thing.

GRANDIER

Which is?

JEANNE

That you were ambitious.

GRANDIER

It's true.

JEANNE

Lacking nobility which blind heaven has refused you, you sought knowledge and riches.

GRANDIER

It's true.

JEANNE

The day you left the pen for the sword, you said, "In three years I will be dead or I will be Captain."

GRANDIER

Again, that's true.

JEANNE

Knowledgeable, you are more so than any other man in the world, rich you can be—Captain, say a word and you shall be.

GRANDIER

I don't understand you, Madam.

JEANNE

Then I will repeat to you what I already told you. Grandier, I love you. Well, is there anything in this world which moves you? This is not the first time I've confessed this to you—and I've seen you implore it on your knees.

GRANDIER

It's true, Madam, but when I implored this confession, I was almost a child. What do you want! When one is young he is ignored or forgotten. I had forgotten that you were rich, that you were noble, that you were named Jeanne de Laubardemont. It took only a word to recall me to reason. That word lit up my spirit, I understood my nothingness compared to your grandeur, and I did right to retire.

JEANNE

Well, hasn't complete reparation been granted, Grandier? You've forgotten, and I remember; you go away, I follow you. You no longer love me, I still love you. Yes, Grandier, as you say, I am rich, I am noble, I am named Jeanne de Laubardemont. Grandier, do you want me for your wife? I am free. I have the authorization to dispose of my hand and here's a commission in blank signed by the Cardinal, which makes my future husband a captain.

GRANDIER

It's a hundred times more than I deserve, Madam. God is my witness that my gratitude to you is profound but I cannot accept it.

JEANNE

You cannot accept it?

GRANDIER

No union is possible without mutual love.

JEANNE

Yes, I still love you, and you don't love me anymore?

GRANDIER

That's not my fault, Madam, something I cannot mention something terrible has passed between our two loves and killed mine.

JEANNE

So you no longer love me, Grandier?

GRANDIER

At least I cannot accept the honor you are doing me.

JEANNE

You no longer love me—confess it openly.

GRANDIER

I will never hate you—that's all I can promise you.

JEANNE

You don't love me any more—say you no longer love me!

GRANDIER

I no longer love you.

JEANNE

(showing a paper to Grandier)

Let me pass, sir—here's the Cardinal's order.

GRANDIER

Pass, Madam.

JEANNE

(one the second step)

Grandier, I am returning to France—have you nothing to say to Ursula de Sable?

GRANDIER

I do! Tell her I am her humble servant, Madam, and that exiled or not, near or far, my last breathe will be for her.

JEANNE

(aside as she leaves)

Oh—it was true then! He loves her! He loves her!

GRANDIER

(watching her leave)

Poor woman.

SCHOMBERG

(at the top of the steps)

Grandier.

GRANDIER

Marshal, sir?

SCHOMBERG

His Eminence, the Cardinal desires to speak to you.

GRANDIER

I cannot leave this post, Milord, I am on watch.

SCHOMBERG

Hey, somebody come take this post for Urbain Grandier for a little while! His Eminence doesn't like to be kept waiting.

GRANDIER

(low to Olivier who reappears)

Mr. de Sourdis—do you understand?

OLIVIER

Oh, my friend, thanks! thanks!

(aloud)

Marshal, Sir, Urbain Grandier is free. I will take the rest of his watch.

SCHOMBERG

Who are you, sir?

OLIVIER

Olivier de Sourdis, Captain in the Poitou Regiment.

SCHOMBERG

Ah, yes! Thanks Captain de Sourdis—come, Grandier.

GRANDIER

Good luck, my Captain.

OLIVIER

Oh! The brave heart!

(Grandier goes up, salutes Schomberg and follows him to the Cardinal's office.)

OLIVIER

And now, not an instant to lose.

(going to the balcony)

Bianca! Bianca!

BIANCA

Is it you, Olivier?

OLIVIER

Yes, yes, it's me.

BIANCA

My God—the moment has come.

OLIVIER

Not only has it come, but we still haven't a moment to lose.

BIANCA

You know that I am locked in.

OLIVIER

Let down a ribbon through the bars of your jalousie.

BIANCA

Wait.

OLIVIER

In the name of heaven, hurry.

BIANCA

Here's the ribbon.

OLIVIER

(attaching the key to the ribbon)

Here's the key.

BIANCA

Someone!

OLIVIER

Don't be afraid, it's a friend.

BIANCA

Then I can open?

OLIVIER

Yes.

(to Nogaret who enters)

Have you the ladder?

NOGARET

Here it is.

OLIVIER

(throwing the ladder to Bianca)

Tie the attachments to the balcony, Bianca and think that it is your life, that is to say more than my life you are risking.

(Nogaret fixes the ladder to the terrace. Bianca attaches the other end to the balcony. Olivier goes up.)

BIANCA

Before God, it's my husband who elopes with me, isn't it?

OLIVIER

(extending his hand)

Before God, it's your husband that you follow—Bianca, come, come!

(The moment she touches the ground, Grandier appears.)

BIANCA

Here I am!

NOGARET

Some one!

OLIVIER

Take her away, Nogaret, take her. If need be, I'll die here.

BIANCA

Olivier! Olivier!

(Nogaret pulls her off.)

OLIVIER

(rushing before Grandier)

Mr. de Sourdis! Mr. de Sourdis! I am captain. I have 100,000 pounds to raise a company—six months liberty before returning to the colors. Oh, Mr. de Sourdis, be as happy as I am—that's all I wish you.

(He rushes past the steps.)

SERGEANT

(entering with two men)

Our Captain, on watch in place of Urbain Grandier?

OLIVIER

Yes, sir, His Eminence called Urbain Grandier and with the authorization of Mr. de Schomberg. I took his place for a moment, as you see.

NEW SENTINEL

The word of order, my Captain?

OLIVIER

Paris and Piedmont.

NEW SENTINEL

The Countersign?

OLIVIER

Don't let any one leave without an order or passport from the Cardinal Duke—good watch, gentlemen.

(He rushes down the stairway and disappears while the Sergeant and the soldiers continue on their way and disappear under the arcade.)

CURTAIN

PROLOGUE

Scene 2

A room in the birthplace of Grandier in the village of Rovère.

L'ABBÉ GRILLAU

I don't know, but it seems to me, while they went on the grand highway to meet our dear Urbain, it seems to me I am a little sleepy. It's astonishing! I always have that feeling when I read my breviary.

GRANDIER

(putting his head through the window)

Better not say that before Milord the Archbishop, Papa Grillau.

L'ABBÉ GRILLAU

Heavens! Grandier! It's you, my child, it's you, my Urbain.

GRANDIER

(entering through the door)

Yes, my good and dear instructor, it's me, your student.

L'ABBÉ GRILLAU

Oh, my student, here's a student who rises a little above his master.

GRANDIER

Not on the side of the heart, at least. Tell me, my friend, nothing bad has happened, why are you alone?

L'ABBÉ GRILLAU

Eh, no, rest assured! Doesn't god watch over good people?

GRANDIER

Then my mother and my brother are well?

L'ABBÉ GRILLAU

Marvelously, they went to meet you.

GRANDIER

They went, you say? My rascally Daniel is here then?

L'ABBÉ GRILLAU

Eh! Certainly, your mother had no sooner received your letter, then, as she doesn't know how to read, the poor dear woman ran to my home so I could read it to her, and I no sooner had read it to her, then she made me write to your brother to run here so the feast would be complete. Oh, he didn't have to be asked twice and he arrived the day before yesterday, your rascally Daniel as you call him.

GRANDIER

So well that they all went to meet me.

L'ABBÉ GRILLAU

Yes.

GRANDIER

On the great highway?

L'ABBÉ GRILLAU

Certainly.

GRANDIER

Oh, that's my fault.

L'ABBÉ GRILLAU

Yours?

GRANDIER

Yes, father, mine. I forgot to tell them one thing, it's that there are memories of youth, mysteries of childhood which run through life from childhood and youth, when one is in a great city like Paris, there is no fatherland, there is a street, that's all—but in a village it's another matter—Virgil said it, father: "O fortunatas numinum!"

L'ABBÉ GRILLAU

Come on, there you go speaking Latin; you know very well that I didn't know what I was teaching you, so that what you know, I no longer know.

GRANDIER

You are right, father.

L'ABBÉ GRILLAU

Never mind! What did that pagan Virgil say—look, explain it to me in French, my child.

GRANDIER

What he said? He said: "Very happy are those born in the country, if they would recognize their luck." I was born in the country, and I recognize my luck.

L'ABBÉ GRILLAU

And you are happy then?

GRANDIER

Oh, yes, indeed happy.

L'ABBÉ GRILLAU

What you said explains Virgil to me, only it doesn't tell me why you didn't meet your mother.

GRANDIER

Why? Listen carefully—because in returning, father, I found, intersecting the road a path, familiar in my childhood, it seemed to me as if my beautiful youth, all crowned with flowers, was waiting for me on this path, making me a sign to follow. Then I left the great highway, the way which leads to cities to follow this hedge of hawthorns and elder trees which leads to graveyards: its there my father and my uncle sleep, my two masters before you. It's the least one can do to visit the dead before the living, and to greet them first, since they left so long ago.

L'ABBÉ GRILLAU

Dear Grandier! Wise as a magi, and with a heart good and pure like a child's.

GRANDIER

It's because my heart has not awakened. It's been twenty years since I played on that path, that I gathered flowers at the foot of the hedge, that I sought insects under the plants or gold or emeralds. Well, for me it was yesterday, there isn't a flower that I don't recognize, not a clump of grass that I don't know by heart, and what I am going to say is going to appear strange to you: not only did I recognize all of that, but it seemed to me that all that had eyes to see me, a voice, a soul to greet me—so much so that when I passed, if I turned about and I listened, I saw the grass and the flowers bow towards each other and I heard them speak in the language of plants and flowers, "You know, sir—it's him."

L'ABBÉ GRILLAU

You see, when you say things like that to me, Urbain, I regret you are not a cure, a monk or even a priest. Ah, the beautiful sermons you would compose—! and how well you would speak of the Good God.

GRANDIER

Oh! The Good God has no need of me to speak his praise, father. When he made the world he filled it with his divinity and everything speaks of his power in creation from the shoot of grass sprouting from the earth up to the sun which makes it flower.

L'ABBÉ GRILLAU

Grandier, my good friend, when I am near you, I feel like the sprout, and you the sun. I love God as I am able, and you as you know.

GRANDIER

And who tells you, father, that the humility of your heart is not more agreeable than the pride of my wit? You envy my science, well, I, Urbain the wise, as you call me, I lean on you, I repose and I feel myself better. Oh, this is so true, my friend—that instead of running after my mother, after my brother, and you know how I love them! This is so true that I remain here near you for I want to tell you things I have not said to the greatest wise men. I want to make a confession to you that I still haven't made to archbishop nor to cardinals.

L'ABBÉ GRILLAU

A confession to me, Urbain?

GRANDIER

Yes, more even than a confession—a case of conscience.

L'ABBÉ GRILLAU

Urbain, sometimes they said, not only were you a Savant, they even said you were a sorcerer. Have you seen the devil, by chance?

GRANDIER

No, I haven't seen him—but perhaps I've given him a hold over me. An English poet that you don't know, father, says that the souls of the Melancholy are easily damned. Suppose I were on the route to damnation!

L'ABBÉ GRILLAU

Oh—Oh, since your trip to Italy? Damn—they say the Italian women are very beautiful.

GRANDIER

I don't know about the Italian women, father for my heart remained in France, and eyes without heart are only a vain rumor which do not retain the memory. No—it was much before this that I doubted.

L'ABBÉ GRILLAU

You doubt, Urbain! You doubt! And what do you doubt?

GRANDIER

Oh—rest assured—in myself.

L'ABBÉ GRILLAU

And what form has this doubt taken?

GRANDIER

On the subject of a power which was given me.

L'ABBÉ GRILLAU

To you?

GRANDIER

But such a power—so great a power, so strange—especially that it can only come from heaven or hell, from God or from the Demon!

L'ABBÉ GRILLAU

Explain yourself, my child.

GRANDIER

I am going to tell you, father, this will be my complete explanation. You know my brother is ten years younger than I am. You even know how much I love him. Also, when he was still a child and when I heard him cry, I went to him right away. Alas, with the child as with the man, there is always suffering at the bottom of the tears. Only the passerby sees the tears and is not disturbed by the suffering, in such a way that if a child is crying, they say—"He's naughty," if it's a man, they say, "He's weak." But I know the contrary, when Daniel wept, I went to him and as I had read in Plato a chapter titled "The Strength of the Will", I took his hands and I looked at him fixedly with absolute will, constant and inflexible so that the sorrow calmed and the tears stopped.

Then all the faculties I had in me enveloped his weakness in their power and soon, really, like a Magi, I saw the sorrow calm and the tears dried up, then a smile rushed like a sweet ray on his face, then his eyes closed, then came sleep, a sleep so sweet, so charming, so peaceable, that it didn't seem like human sleep to me. One day then, this sleep appeared to me so full of ineffable beatitude, that I seemed to see the soul of the child behind his partially opened lips. Then I spoke to him as one speaks, not to sleep but to ecstasy. Father, he answered me.

L'ABBÉ GRILLAU

Completely asleep as he was?

GRANDIER

Yes, completely asleep—but we are not yet at the strange, unheard of, miraculous thing—it's that the material obstacles had disappeared and that from a distance through the walls, he saw as he slept.

L'ABBÉ GRILLAU

Grandier!

GRANDIER

Listen right to the end. I asked him—it was the first question that came to mind—I asked him where our mother was—then, without leaving his place, without rising from the armchair in which he was seated, "Wait brother, I will find her." Then, his eyes still closed: "Ah," he continue, "wait I see her, wait, she's gathering boxwood for soup from the lake, then she will go get it blessed at the church. Heavens, it's not the Abbé Grillau who is blessing it, it's the Vicar—ah—there she is leaving the church—she's stopping to talk with my Uncle Claude—he's giving her a little gold cross and she's leaving him—she's coming—open the door, brother." I run to the door, my mother was on the sill. She'd been gathering boxwood for soup from the lake, she'd been to the church to have it blessed, it was the vicar who blessed it and not you. Fifty paces from here she met my Uncle Claude—and she held in her hand the little gold cross he had given her—which she still wears at her neck.

L'ABBÉ GRILLAU

You are sure of what you say there, Grandier?

GRANDIER

Twenty times I retested it, and he's never mistaken.

L'ABBÉ GRILLAU

Have you spoken to him about this?

GRANDIER

To Daniel? No—you alone. God and you know about this.

L'ABBÉ GRILLAU

Now, Urbain, isn't it your brother and not you who does this? I've heard tell there are children and old folks—who have double vision—and I explain it this way—children are near the cradle and old folks are near the tomb—infants and old folks are near God who is the beginning and end of all things.

GRANDIER

I would say, as you do, father, if Daniel was the sole person on whom I had tried my power.

L'ABBÉ GRILLAU

You've tried it on others beside him?

GRANDIER

Listen—this is where I really fear to have fallen into sin—this is where I tremble to see the finger of an evil spirit.

L'ABBÉ GRILLAU

Speak.

GRANDIER

Six years later, I was in Bordeaux, I was getting out of college. I fell in love with a young girl, I cannot say her name—now, you understand why, she was of the nobility. Despite the difference in our situations she encouraged my love. Yes, in the midst of our happy hours which were nonetheless chaste, father, it sometimes happened that sudden sorrows passed over her face—which she forced herself to hide from me, but which despite her efforts, were as visible to me as the shadows of clouds running over wheat. Twenty times, I asked her what was wrong and why she was suddenly becoming so somber—but she always refused to reply to me.

One morning after having left her, left her late at night and pressed by useless questions, I received a letter from her forbidding me to see her again. I read and reread this letter, and having the instinct and perhaps the pride of a lover, I thought I recognized a certain hesitation in the style, a shade of trembling in the handwriting, I concluded that this letter had been imposed on her, that this letter, written by her was dictated by another. The same evening, I should have returned to her for a few days had passed without our seeing each other—she lived in an isolated house near the river. Night came. I hid myself in the alder trees and willows which soaked their branches in the water.

At ten o'clock, I saw a man enter her house who only left at midnight. It seemed to me I had never seen this man, who anyway hid himself in a great cloak. The window of room of the one I loved gave on a garden where we had often strolled together. I climbed over the wall of this garden. The window was open—but the curtains were drawn. I climbed the length of the trellis and reached the balcony. She was seated before a table her head in her hands—at the noise I made climbing over the balustrade, she raised her face. I was going to be surprised scaling a window like a thief. She was going to call out, scream, perhaps—I extended my arm towards her, and without touching her, without saying a word, solely through power of will gushing from all my pores, I stopped her. She remained with her view fixed, immobile like a statue. Then I recognized this strange sleep I had already studied in my brother. But instead of being calm and sweet as Daniel was, her sleep was agitated, panting, almost convulsive. I wanted to know if she would also speak—and I questioned her. First, she obstinately kept silent, but to my order, she yielded. Ah, why didn't she remain quiet! My conscience would not be charged today with such a terrible secret. Father, I wasn't mistaken, the letter I had received had been dictated. She had written it despite herself, obeying a power stronger than hers. This man I had seen leaving her house was her lover—and this...

(lowering his voice)

...incestuous lover was her father!

L'ABBÉ GRILLAU

My God!

GRANDIER

Hush! Did I say it? At least I didn't name the person, right?

L'ABBÉ GRILLAU

And you haven't seen her since that time?

GRANDIER

At least I've never sought to see her.

L'ABBÉ GRILLAU

You are right, Grandier, there's something strange in such a work. Where does it come from? I am as ignorant as you. Did you have some blessed object on you when you had these experiences?

GRANDIER

The last time, I had this holy medal on my throat, given me by my mother on the day of my departure.

L'ABBÉ GRILLAU

Then it's no evil spirit in you, since this blessed medal would have been more powerful than such a spirit.

GRANDIER

What is it, then?

L'ABBÉ GRILLAU

Listen, Grandier, do you still want to clear up your doubts?

GRANDIER

Oh, yes father, I wish to.

L'ABBÉ GRILLAU

Well, let's attempt it today—the sooner the better—I don't have the pretension to be a holy man, but I am an honest man who defies Satan, Beelzebub, Astorath, and all the infamous legion—you will show me this power on your brother, at the same time I will say an act of faith. If there's some devil at the bottom of all this, however well hidden he may be, he'll have to betray himself.

GRANDIER

Hush! I hear some noise.

DANIEL

(entering)

Mother! Mother! It doesn't surprise me we didn't see Grandier come. He's here.

GRANDIER

Daniel, dear child!

DANIEL

(running)

Hello, hello, brother. Oh! I embraced him first.

MME. GRANDIER

(entering)

What are you saying here? Grandier here? But how did you pass, my child. Jesus, my God! It's true. Here he is.

(hanging on his neck)

Oh! My God! My God!

DANIEL

I loan him to you—you'll give him back? Ah, it was you who kept him to yourself, Father Grillau? You're going to catch it for confiscating the soldiers of the king to your profit.

(opening the Abbé's Breviary)

Te Deum Laudamus.

GRANDIER

What are you doing, rascal?

DANIEL

Heavens! He is returned, I am chanting the *Te Deum*.

GRANDIER

Yes, returned and quite happy, mother for I didn't tell you everything in my letter. You see how egotistical I am. I delayed eight hours to share my happiness with you—I wanted you to learn it from me.

MME. GRANDIER

Oh—whatever you do is well done, go on, tell us now, since you are here.

GRANDIER

Mother, I'm a captain.

MME. GRANDIER

You've succeeded? And who made you captain, my God?

GRANDIER

The Cardinal.

DANIEL

What? You are captain? Captain like Mr. de Sourdis? You are going to have embroidered clothes like him?

GRANDIER

I have a hundred thousand pounds to raise a company.

MME. GRANDIER

And who gave you this hundred thousand pounds?

GRANDIER

The Cardinal.

DANIEL

Long live the Cardinal!

GRANDIER

That is not all.

MME. GRANDIER

What do you mean, that's not all?

GRANDIER

No, I've kept the best part of last, mother.

MME. GRANDIER

Tell us quickly then!

GRANDIER

Six months leave, mother, six months to spend near you.

MME. GRANDIER

And who gave you that?

GRANDIER

The Cardinal.

MME. GRANDIER

Saintly man!

DANIEL

(shouting at the top of his voice)

Long live the Cardinal.

(singing and causing the Abbé Grillau to turn)

Tra-la-la, Tra-la-la.

GRANDIER

Why what are you doing?

DANIEL

Heavens! When I'm happy, I dance. That's my way of praising God.

MME. GRANDIER

(looking around her)

Ah! Grandier, my child, how poor you are going to find this house now.

GRANDIER

Poor mother! Poor house where you gave an example of all your virtues, the house where you were a chaste, spouse, good mother! Poor chapel, church, temple, mother! If all this gold they gave me was mine, I would encase the sill that your foot blessed with gold.

MME. GRANDIER

All the same, you see, my child, I've made it as beautiful as possible, this poor house! Here are the beautiful flowers that you love, the beautiful materials you sent me from Italy. I wanted it to smile at you, since it was going to see you again.

GRANDIER

Yes, here indeed are my flowers and my materials, but it seems to me they lack one thing.

MME. GRANDIER

Yes, that beautiful Madonna you sent me from de Suze, where you had it copied, you said during your garrison there. Heaven, here she is—what did you expect I would do with this gold brocade if not make a veil for her.

(She discovers the Madonna.)

GRANDIER

Ah!

DANIEL

Grandier, don't you think your Madonna de Suze resembles a bit, even a great deal, Miss de Sable?

GRANDIER

Hush, child, let's not laugh about holy things. Mother, you believe what I've told you, don't you? Well, no indeed, there remains one last joy to reveal to you—but first, tell me—how's her health?

MME. GRANDIER

Isn't one's health always good when one is happy?

GRANDIER

Is she happy?

MME. GRANDIER

Almost as happy as I.

GRANDIER

Has it been a long time since you saw her?

MME. GRANDIER

Last Sunday at Mass.

DANIEL

And I, yesterday morning, with her father.

GRANDIER

Is she still beautiful?

MME. GRANDIER

Like an angel.

GRANDIER

Mother, she loves me, she is free, she's waiting for me.

MME. GRANDIER

She is even more my daughter than you are my son, for you only told me this today, she told me a month ago. But where am I—I am forgetting you've made a long journey, that you are hot, thirsty, hungry perhaps—I am forgetting you want to see her again—come Daniel, come help me.

GRANDIER

(in response to a glance from the Abbey)

No, mother, allow me to keep him.

MME. GRANDIER

Well, at least give me a hug.

GRANDIER

Oh, yes—never enough, mother.

(Mme. Grandier leaves.)

DANIEL

Oh, I know quite well why you are keeping me. Go on! I know quite well of whom you wish to speak!

GRANDIER

Ah, you know that, do you?

DANIEL

You want me to talk about Miss de Sable, you keep me, 'cause I told you I met her yesterday.

GRANDIER

Well, yes—what did she say to you, dear child?

DANIEL

She asked me news of you, she told me I resemble you, and she kissed me on the face.

GRANDIER

(embracing him at the same time)

Is that all?

DANIEL

Then she showed me her flowers, her birds, the Château, the park—and she said to me, "You know all that is his?"

GRANDIER

Dear Ursula! Then she still loves me?

DANIEL

Oh that? She didn't tell me that, no. But I saw it.

GRANDIER

Then you know the park?

DANIEL

Yes.

GRANDIER

The Castle.

DANIEL

Yes.

GRANDIER

The apartment.

DANIEL

Yes.

GRANDIER

Consequently, you can tell me where she is at the moment.

DANIEL

Me?

GRANDIER

Yes—what she'd going.

DANIEL

How can you expect me to tell you that?

GRANDIER

What she thinks even.

DANIEL

Ah, really, why I am not a sorcerer! I have good eyes, it's true, but still, I cannot see here to Sable!

GRANDIER

Ah, if you really wanted to—

DANIEL

What do you mean? If you really wanted to, I could see a place far from here?

GRANDIER

Yes.

DANIEL

Oh!

GRANDIER

And you could tell me what Ursula is doing.

DANIEL

Come on, you are mocking me, brother.

GRANDIER

No—give me your hands.

DANIEL

Here they are.

GRANDIER

Look at me.

DANIEL

I am looking at you.

GRANDIER

That's right.

DANIEL

Oh! Grandier—I recall—Grandier, it's like when I was a child, and when I wept, you consoled me and made me go to sleep. Ah—

(Closing his eyes.)

GRANDIER

Here, father—see how he sleeps.

GRANDIER

My word, it's true.

(The face of the child, animated and smiling as it was—becomes calm.)

GRANDIER

Daniel!

DANIEL

(with a voice or tone difference from that he had when he was awake)

Brother?

GRANDIER

Dream what I want.

DANIEL

Yes, since I read it in your thoughts. You want me to give you news of Miss de Sable, don't you?

GRANDIER

Yes, do you see?

DANIEL

Open my eyes, brother?

GRANDIER

Wait.

(He passes his hand in front of the boy's eyes which become fixed as in an ecstasy.)

DANIEL

I see.

GRANDIER

Look—do you see Ursula?

DANIEL

No—not yet—I'm looking for her.

GRANDIER

Do you think you will find her?

DANIEL

Certainly! I am going to go everywhere I was with her yesterday. Ah—first of all—there—I am in the park.

GRANDIER

Is she there?

DANIEL

No, she isn't.

GRANDIER

Go into the house, then.

DANIEL

That's what I am doing—I am going up the steps—oh, my God!

GRANDIER

What?

DANIEL

Why, you would say something unusual is happening at the Château.

GRANDIER

And what is happening? Let's see—look.

DANIEL

The servants are running about, weeping—the chapel bells are ringing.

GRANDIER

Oh! Daniel, you are mistaken—look, listen carefully?

DANIEL

Oh—I'm not mistaken.

GRANDIER

But Ursula—do you see her?

DANIEL

No, no, I don't see her.

GRANDIER

Neither in the park nor in the Château? Why where is she then?

DANIEL

Wait, wait, I am going to follow them.

GRANDIER

Who?

DANIEL

The priests.

GRANDIER

The priests?

DANIEL

Yes, they are entering the Château.

GRANDIER

What are they going to do there?

DANIEL

Wait, wait! They are going up the stairway. They are opening a door—its' the door of her chamber—ah, poor Urbain! I see her, I see her.

GRANDIER

My God! My God! What's happening to her? What's she doing?

DANIEL

She's rising in her bed, she wants to speak, she's falling back—she's dying, she's dead!

GRANDIER

(rushing out of the room)

Oh! Ursula! Ursula!

MME. GRANDIER

(running in)

Who's calling? Who's shouting! I heard Urbain's voice.

(noticing Daniel collapsed in Father Grillau's arms)

Daniel, my child, Daniel!

DANIEL

(waking up)

What's going on?

GRANDIER

Take this child away, take him—and I will tell you—everything.

BLACKOUT

PROLOGUE

Scene 3

A chamber in the Château de Sable's Mortuary room. Ursula is lying pale and motionless on her bed. She has the crown of virgins, a crucifix on her breast, the children of the choir and the Deacons surround her bed. The servants of the house are on their knees in the room! The scene shift occurs on the singing of the De Profundis.

PRIEST

From the depths of the abyss, arms convulsed by sadness, I cried to the sublime Master "Pity on us, pity, Lord."

(Religious music.)

PRIEST

(returning)

Pity for the ephemeral child whose soft limpid eye is shut on its mother's breast knowing nothing, not even you.

Pity for the old folks who doubt under the bending weight of years, and who towards, the end of their way, have forgotten even you.

(Religious music. Urbain Grandier appears and falls on his knees among the servants.)

PRIEST

(starting up again after having seen Urbain)

Pity especially for the hermit who follows the sad path, the last who remains on earth, Lord, he is the most wretched.

(Religious music. The priests throw holy water on the dead woman and go off. The servants leave one after another.)

(Urbain approaches the foot of the bed.)

GRANDIER

It was to live with you, chaste child, pure virgin, that I wanted to conquer the honors and riches of the earth, and now, rushing to receive the crown of angels, you've gone to wait for me in heaven. Henceforth it is to heaven that I must offer my vows, it's in heaven I am going to rejoin you. Goodbye to the joys of this world, goodbye to all the baubles, to all the symbols of ambition. The realm of heaven is to the poor body, to the humble spirit—the realm of heaven is for those who pray, and not those who fight, to those who bend not, those who struggle.

(Madam Grandier and Daniel enter at this point.)

GRANDIER

Then away with the floating plume.

(throwing away his felt hat)

The clashing arms.

(throwing away his sword)

The symbols of command.

(throwing away his scarf)

Ursula, before this altar, where the mysterious sacrifice of death has just been accomplished, your fiancé renounces, not life, but the world. God alone, who gives life can dispose of it—and the only suicide worthy of the Christian—is the monastery. Ursula, from the moment you breathed your last sigh, Captain Grandier has ceased to exist to make way for the monk, Urbain. To him solitude, to him prayer, to him haircloth. Damn Daniel, pardon, mother! Something more powerful than you has torn me from you.

(Mme. Grandier and Daniel lean against and support each other.)

MME. GRANDIER

My child.

DANIEL

Grandier!

GRANDIER

Daniel, mother! Goodbye.

(tearing himself from their arms, and going to fall that the feet of the dead girl)

Yours, Ursula, yours in this world and the next.

MME. GRANDIER

(raising her arms to heaven)

So be it!

CURTAIN

ACT I

Scene 4

The Church of Loudon.

MIGNON

Damn, you understand Count, it's a serious thing to take the veil, especially since the nun is a foreigner—and one wants to act properly.

MAURIZIO

Eh, my dear sir, you are in proper order, here's your license, here's the donation of six thousand Roman schillings given by the countess Albizzio to your convent, or rather to the Ursuline convent of which you are the director. Moreover, here is for you the reversion of the curate of St. Pierre de Loudon—with a benefice of 3,000 pounds, to make you patient. As to the rest, the thing is very simple, my God. My sister, still a minor was kidnapped from her maternal home by a French officer, who after we had found her place of retreat with the Ursulines of Loudon, abandoned her and ran from Italy for his pleasure. Anyway, it seems to me that Bianca won't resist you, right?

MIGNON

No, Count, now that she knows Mr. de Sourdis no longer loves her. On the contrary, she seems no longer patient to wait for the event which previously she dreaded so much.

MAURIZIO

And, tell me, once taken the vows are as indissoluble in France as they are in Italy, right?

MIGNON

Yes, Count.

MAURIZIO

Oh! It's that you have a devil of a parliament.

MIGNON

It cannot interfere with ecclesiastical affairs.

MAURIZIO

So that, when and if she learns—as one must assume everything, when she learns we have deceived her regarding Mr. de Sourdis, that he still loves her.

MIGNON

Mr. de Sourdis still loves your sister?

MAURIZIO

Eh! My God! Who told you that? I suppose that's all. How do you expect me to know in France, what he's doing in Italy? They wrote me he's going to marry the richest heiress in Turin—I believe it, and you must believe it, too, until you have proof to the contrary.

MIGNON

I believe it, Count.

MAURIZIO

So that, were she to learn we are mistaken, and that consequently we had deceived her—once her vows are taken—

MIGNON

There's no way back—no, Count, there's no example—

MAURIZIO

Thanks much—that's enough. She's unaware I am here, right?

MIGNON

She believes you are in Mantua. And as even yesterday, we gave her a letter from you which is supposed to come from Italy.

MAURIZIO

Good. I am there, behind this pillar—no one knows me except you, the Superior and your Vicar, Barre—I shall not appear unless it is absolutely necessary. Ah—some one is opening—don't waste time, eh?

MIGNON

(returning)

The Count can rest easy. All the required orders have been given—and all precautions have been taken so there will be no delay.

(He goes off.)

MAURIZIO

Fine! That man is an ambitious subaltern who will do anything to obtain the daughter of a great family for the convent he directs. With what pleasure and pride he enumerated all his penitents! Does he, by chance, think I would have put my sister in a convent that was not noble?

BAILIFF

(approaching the Count)

You are a stranger, sir?

MAURIZIO

Yes, sir. I desire to be present in her taking the veil.

BAILIFF

And while waiting, you are looking over our church?

MAURIZIO

Yes, sir.

BAILIFF

Oh! It's a magnificent church! How do you find it?

MAURIZIO

Not bad.

BAILIFF

What do you mean, not bad?

MAURIZIO

Doubtless for a small town.

BAILIFF

Oh! Oh! Loudon is not precisely a little town, sir, anyway. It has a bailiwick—I am the bailiff.

MAURIZIO

I am your servant, sir.

(He moves away.)

BAILIFF

It is I who am yours—I was saying there's a bailiwick, an abbey, an Ursuline convent, where we count the most considerable names in our province—a young lady from Fasili—a cousin of the Cardinal-Duke, two ladies from Barbenis, of the house of Nogaret, a young miss from Barace, a—

(noticing that he's speaking by himself)

Well—he's quite polite—this gentleman!

(going to Urbain's mother, who is kneeling by a chair)

Ah—there you are, Mme. Grandier!

MME. GRANDIER

Sir, sir.

BAILIFF

Is Urbain giving a sermon?

MME. GRANDIER

No, sir.

BAILIFF

Heavens! And why's that? Still, for God's sake, it's his affair. Good, here I am swearing in the church! But as it is in praise of a Saint, the good God will pardon me, for your son is a saint—at least all our women say so.

DANIEL

(entering)

They don't say as much of you, Bailiff.

BAILIFF

Of me? What are they saying of me?

DANIEL

Oh! I'd gladly repeat it to you but I dare not in a church.

BAILIFF

Have you seen this little wise guy?

DANIEL

Hug me, mama.

(Mme. Grandier hugs him.)

BAILIFF

It is true, Mme. Grandier, that your son hasn't seen you or his brother since he took his vows?

MME. GRANDIER

You know, what a great sorrow determined Grandier to become a priest. The chains which attached him to the world were not loosened, they were broken, and if we had seen him in the course of the first year, he told us he feared the sight of us would only raise his sorrows above his resignation.

BAILIFF

And when a year has gone by he will make his profession?

MME. GRANDIER

Today it is exactly a year. Daniel and I, indeed hope to embrace him today.

DANIEL

Oh, don't worry dear mother—I will enter the monastery. I am a man—no one will pay attention to me, and once he's hugged me he'll have to embrace you.

MME. GRANDIER

I know I am in his heart as he is in mine, and I am patient, my child.

BAILIFF

You know your son has not wasted his time? After only a year in orders here he is superior of a convent.

DANIEL

Heavens! He was already captain of his company—it seems to me the first was worth more—but, wait, Monsieur le Bailiff.

BAILIFF

What?

DANIEL

There's your wife who can't find a place to sit here.

BAILIFF

Oh! Bah! Bah! Bah!

DANIEL

No—word of honor, I think she needs you. Ah, if it was Simone, the dressmaker, you wouldn't have to be asked twice.

BAILIFF

Well, you shut up, little wise guy! Well, you shut up!

(He runs to his wife.)

DANIEL

(approaching his mother)

Mother.

MME. GRANDIER

Child, you are preventing me from praying.

DANIEL

I want to tell you something—do you know what?

MME. GRANDIER

What?

DANIEL

Mr. de Sourdis is in France.

MME. GRANDIER

In France, but they said he was going to marry in Italy?

DANIEL

Well, no—he is in France! He is in Paris—he's not going to get married. It seems he still loves Miss Bianca, he went back to Italy looking for her; then they deceived the poor girl by telling her Mr. de Sourdis was in love with someone else—so now she's going to take vows which she will probably repent all her life.

MME. GRANDIER

And who told you this?

DANIEL

Oh, my God—one of my friends to whom Mr. de Sourdis has always been very good—and as Mr. de Sourdis doesn't trust anyone but him, first of all, because he thinks that as he is a child, no one will watch him—he sent him a letter begging him to pass this letter to Miss Bianca before she takes her vows.

MME. GRANDIER

And has he passed this letter Mr. de Sourdis sent him?

DANIEL

No, not yet, mama—

MME. GRANDIER

Why?

DANIEL

Damn, mama—he's afraid of doing evil and as you are a saintly woman, and can give only good advice, he begged me to consult you.

MME. GRANDIER

Tell him to give it to her, my child. If it is true, they are deceiving this young girl, if it is true they are forcing a vocation on her by lying to her, it would be a crime to keep her unaware that Mr. de Sourdis still loves her.

DANIEL

That's fine. Now he'll have a quiet conscience.

(Commotion in the church. All the assistants take their places. The organ can be heard behind the chorus. The nuns sing *Salve Regina*. All the bells sound. Bianca enters leaning on the shoulder of one nun, sustained by another and followed by the Abbess. On each side of the abbess, Mignon and Barace. A large group of nuns.)

ASSISTANTS

(standing on chairs)

Ah—there she is! There she is! You know she's an Italian. Oh, how pale she is! Damn, they say she's being forced, the poor girl. If it was me, I would say no. That would get you a long way! They cannot force you. No, no, no—but since her lover has abandoned her—on the contrary, and that's why she's going to be a nun! Ah, poor child.

SWISS

Silence.

DANIEL

(sliding near Bianca)

Take this letter.

(putting it in her hand)

Take it.

(Bianca takes it mechanically and keep it in her folded hands. The singing and organ music cease.)

MIGNON

Come, my child—you must remove all these worldly pomps—nothing must remain on you, as nothing must remain in you which belongs to this world and therefore to the Demon.

BIANCA

(holding out her hands as they remove her bracelets and lace, then her neck so they can remove her necklace and her head so they can remove her veil.)

Do it, my sister.

(Everything is removed from the novice as the organ sounds and the nuns chant.)

DANIEL

(low, approaching Bianca)

Read it!

MIGNON

What's your name, my daughter?

BIANCA

Bianca dei Albizzio.

MIGNON

What do you request?

BIANCA

That the church receive me in its bosom.

DANIEL

Read it!

MIGNON

Do you promise to answer truly?

BIANCA

I promise.

DANIEL

Will you read it—it's from him!

MIGNON

(pointing to Daniel)

Take away that child who's messing up the ceremony.

BIANCA

From him.

(looking at the letter)

This letter! His writing! My God!

MIGNON

What's wrong with you, my daughter?

BIANCA

Nothing! I ask a moment to meditate.

(going to the foot of the cross)

Pardon me, my God, if a profane thought just entered my heart at the moment I was going to belong to you—but didn't a voice just murmur in my ear, "It's from him?"

ABBESS

It seems to me someone gave her a letter.

MIGNON

Go to her, sister, and beg her—

ABBESS

I am Jeanne de Laubardemont, I am the Superior of the Convent of the Ursulines. I don't beg, I order or I take—

MIGNON

Then I am going myself.

(He approaches Bianca, who has read the letter from de Sourdis—she watches him to come to her.)

MAURIZIO

(aside)

What's going on?

MME. GRANDIER

Did they give her the letter, Daniel?

DANIEL

Yes, mother, they gave her the letter.

BIANCA

(to Mignon looking him in the face)

Father—you are a man of God, and as such you cannot lie—right? Everything they've told me is true?

MIGNON

What subject are you asking me about?

BIANCA

Is it true that Mr. de Sourdis has forgotten me, isn't it?

MIGNON

My daughter.

BIANCA

Is he in Italy?

MIGNON

My daughter!

BIANCA

And that he's going to get married in Turin? All this is really true—for in the face of God, you wouldn't dare to lie—reply to me—that all this is true.

MIGNON

My daughter—

TWO NUNS

(returning to Bianca)

They are waiting for you, my sister.

BIANCA

That's fine, I am here—continue to question me—father—I am ready to respond.

MIGNON

(starting over)

Bianca dei Albizzio—do you promise to tell the truth?

BIANCA

(in a voice almost threatening)

I promise!

MIGNON

Is it, by your own free will you are here?

BIANCA

(in a loud voice)

No! It's because they lied to me.

(Commotion in the assembly)

CONFUSED VOICES

She said no! She said no! She said they lied to her.

BAILIFF

(to his wife)

Did you hear that, Madame?

WOMAN

Yes, she said no. They deceived her, poor girl.

MIGNON

Do be quiet!

(to Bianca in a low voice)

Reflect on what you said, my child.

(aloud)

Do you vow poverty, obedience and celibacy?

BIANCA

(in a strong voice)

No!

MIGNON

My daughter—pull yourself together and listen to me—you didn't understand me.

BIANCA

Oh, yes, I did! You asked me if I promised God poverty, obedience and celibacy—I understood you and I answer—no, no, no—I promise nothing.

ABBESS

(laughing)

Good! Yet one more soul which is ruined.

(Murmur and tumult)

NUNS

Sister, sister!

PRIEST

Daughter—

BIANCA

Yes, this is a great scandal, I know it, but it falls back on the heads of those who deceived me. I call on you all who hear me—to all those of you who have loved even once in their lives. They told me the man I loved no longer loved me, they told me he had left France for fear of seeing me again, they told me he was in Italy, that he was going to marry another woman, and little by little, sorrow by sorrow, despair by despair—they prostrated me at the feet of God. I thought I had lost everything on earth and I asked heaven to give me faith instead of love. But they lied, he still loves me, he is in France. He's coming back. He tells me to keep myself for him, he tells me not to take vows, he tells me --.

(They force her to her knees and try to put a veil over her head but she tears it off and in so doing, her hair falls, a nun approaches her with scissors. Bianca hesitates an instant, then says.)

BIANCA

Help! Help!

(Then she escapes from those around her and comes to the front of the stage, shouting).

BIANCA

No! No! No! I don't want them to cut my hair! I don't wish it. No! No! No! I don't wish it!

(Tumult, great noise.)

OLIVIER

Bianca! Bianca!

BIANCA

It's him! It's his voice. Let me pass.

OLIVIER

(in the church)

Bianca—is there still time? Oh, I will fight for you against the entire world, even God.

(drawing his sword)

MAURIZIO

Sword in its scabbard, sir, if you don't want your hand cut off for having drawn a sword in a church.

OLIVIER

Maurizio! Here!

BIANCA

My brother in France!

MAURIZIO

I am the brother of this young girl and I represent all her family—who vow her to God through my voice, and here is an order from the Cardinal Duke which orders completion of the ceremony not withstanding any opposition.

(to the soldiers who are in the church)

Do your duty.

OLIVIER

Oh! Nogaret! Barace, help me! If there is to be force, we must take her away.

BIANCA

(going to embrace the cross)

My God, my God, my only hope is in you!

GRANDIER

(appearing and putting his hand on Bianca)

Who wishes to give God a spouse in spite of herself and in spite of him?

ALL

(recoiling)

Urbain Grandier! Urbain Grandier!

(Tumult!)

BIANCA

Oh—be my support, my upholder, my savior.

GRANDIER

Let Mr. de Sourdis pass.

(The guards hesitate)

MAURIZIO

I speak in the name of the Cardinal Duke—take care!

GRANDIER

And I, I speak in the name of God—let Mr. de Sourdis pass.

(The ranks of the soldiers open.)

OLIVIER

Grandier, my friend!

GRANDIER

(putting Bianca in de Sourdis' hands)

Daughter, you would have made a bad nun—God prefers that you be an honest woman. Go!

ABBESS

(aside, watching Grandier)

The man is too handsome to be an earthly creature. He must be an angel or a demon!

BLACKOUT

ACT I

Scene 5

Grandier's cell. The cell of a painter, musician and savant—as well as of a monk. The portrait of the Virgin seen at Urbain's home and which is none other than the portrait of Ursula de Sable. A bright ray of daylight penetrates the cell through the window covered with flowers.

GRANDIER

(seated and giving a letter to a monk)

This letter, you see, my brother, is for Mr. Escoubleau de Sourdis, Archbishop of Bordeaux. I have given him an account of my conduct in this affair. I've told him of the most minute details which have occurred in the Convent of the Ursulines. I told him that this forced taking of the veil was a sacrilege—it is important that this letter arrive as soon as possible. I may be forestalled by some enemy. The messenger shall not stop en route as time is absolutely essential, and will go directly to the Archbishop. Go, my brother.

(The monk bows and leaves.)

GRANDIER

My mother was there, Daniel was also there. My arms opened, despite myself to hug them to my heart. Poor Grandier, you are still weak! O, my God! Why are you confusing the love I bear them with the memory of another love? No, I won't see them yet—I would talk to them of her—and it's quite enough to speak of her to you, my God, who made her an angel and have her seated by your side. She knew them, she loved them, if I see them again, it's as if I saw her—she—oh, no, I won't see them—not yet at least.

MONK

Your commission is carried out, reverend father and the messenger is going to leave this very instant.

GRANDIER

Did you return only to tell me that?

MONK

I returned to tell you that the Bailiff asked to speak to you, reverend, sir.

GRANDIER

The Bailiff.

MONK

He says he has an important commission to discharge to you.

BAILIFF

(at the door)

Do I disturb you, reverend?

GRANDIER

Not at all.

BAILIFF

In that case, I will return another day.

GRANDIER

Come in, I beg you.

BAILIFF

Ah, here I am in the sanctum sanctorum. It's here you write the beautiful sermons that you recite from the pulpit, it's here you compose that beautiful music that they sing us in greeting, it's here again that you paint those beautiful pictures which foreigners visiting our churches think we get from Venice, Florence, and Rome.

GRANDIER

Sir, I have not only left the world, I brought with me into this solitude a faithful friend and assiduous companion.

BAILIFF

The fact is you have the right to preach to others. From my bed chamber, I see the window of your cell—well, whenever I wake up at night, if I look this way, your lamp is burning. Don't you ever sleep?

GRANDIER

I sleep a little at least.

BAILIFF

In a way that you are busy—ceaselessly?

GRANDIER

Time is a serpent which kills those who do not know how to employ it, and which caresses those who put it to profit.

BAILIFF

And you don't think such occupations are a little profane?

GRANDIER

No, sir—for I believe that the Lord is present in all things, and you know, he who believes, sees. Me, I see God everywhere. The problem I ask of science, that is God. The melody I look for in music, that's God. The beautiful ideal that I dream of in painting, that's God. All which is great and good comes from God and returns to God. But you have, you say, an important communication for me, sir?

BAILIFF

Ah, first off—I wish to congratulate you on what you did today in church regarding that poor girl they wanted to make into a nun despite herself.

GRANDIER

Then you don't blame me for coming to her aid?

BAILIFF

Oh, no—quite the contrary, nor do our women. Ah, if you could listen at every door, I am sure there is not now, except perhaps at the Convent of the Ursulines, a single gossip in all of Loudon who doesn't sing your praises. Ah, take care, if this continues, I think you'll draw on yourself yet more than you can imagine.

GRANDIER

So you find I did what I ought to do?

BAILIFF

Yes, yes, yes—although there's a certain danger in it. You know the thing could turn out badly for you?

GRANDIER

Ah! Ah! You think of my disobedience, or rather my opposition to the orders of the Cardinal?

BAILIFF

No, I don't greatly fear big enemies, I only fear little ones. The Cardinal has too much to do to occupy himself with you—but watch out for Mignon, the Director of our Devotees from whom you took a dowry of 6,000 shillings—watch out for Barre, his vicar—they have time to spare, those two, and if they employ it to cause you mischief, it won't astonish me.

GRANDIER

Is this the communication you wished to make me, sir? In that case, I think you from the depths of my heart for being concerned about me.

BAILIFF

No, that's not it yet. I come, as you are not only a saintly man, but also a learned doctor, Monsieur Grandier—I came to share with you certain rumors that have begun to run about the town and to ask you if you believe in their reality.

GRANDIER

Ah, you wish to speak of these apparitions seen lately in certain parts of the old Château of Loudon.

BAILIFF

Yes, and that despite the proximity to our convent of the Ursulines.

GRANDIER

You attach importance to the gossip of old women, sir? You are very good.

BAILIFF

Eh! Eh! Very intelligent and in no way timid men have assured me, reverend, that passing the day near an opening giving on the cellar of the convent they heard something like groanings, something like wailings, something like prayers, while others passing the night near the cloister, told me they have seen—oh. seen with their own eyes! Large white shapes crossing the terrace, and making threatening gestures with their veils to the curious.

GRANDIER

Threatening gestures with their veils aren't very dangerous signs, sir.

BAILIFF

Then you don't believe in apparitions?

DANIEL

(passing through the window and going to hide behind the curtain)

Well, if you don't believe it, brother, I am going to convince you.

BAILIFF

It seems to met that even in the holy books—ah, you don't believe it?

GRANDIER

I don't say that, sir. I believe in all the facts contained in the Old and New Testaments and even some which have been reported in the lives of the pagans. Then, I see, in the Bible, that the ghost of Samuel, evoked by the Witch of Endor, appeared to Saul. I see in the Gospels, that Christ appeared to Magdalena. Moreover, I see in Plutarch, that at Sardis, the spectre of Caesar appeared to Brutus, and announced to him his second apparition at Philippi would be his defeat and his death. I would then do ill. I, poor soldier of yesterday, poor monk of today, to struggle against such authorities and I believe in these apparitions: the first two as articles of faith, the third as a historic fact. But I believe that so to trouble the usual order of nature, I think that—for the dead once abed in their tombs to arise—I think that it's necessary that God, that is to say, the supreme unity, the supreme power, the supreme intelligence—must have powerful motives.

This motive was powerful at the time of Saul, since it affected the life and happiness of a nation, so the shade of Samuel came to contest the madness of its King. This motive was powerful in regard to Magdalena, since it was a question, though the means of one of the holy women who had assisted at his death, of proclaiming the resurrection of Christ. This motive was powerful—vis-à-vis Brutus, since it was advice given to the murderer by the victim, that political murder is infamous and odious equally with other murders, but even useless. These are the apparitions, I believe in, sir, and that because they have a great end of humanity, of faith or of doctrine, but as to apparitions whose end is to scare of the curious from an air hole or a quarry, or the ruins of an old castle, no—in these I confess to you, I believe very little or not at all.

BAILIFF

My dear Grandier, you speak like a book, and even I will say there are many books that don't speak like you. But, if these apparitions are confirmed in my capacity of bailiff, I have certain responsibilities to my fellow citizens—what should I do?

GRANDIER

You will come find me one evening, sir. I will remove this palm from the wall, which was brought me from Jerusalem and which, when it was attached to its shaft, shaded the divine tomb of our Lord. And, this blessed bough in hand, I myself will go, confident in the purity of my heart and in the assistance of God to assure myself of the truth.

BAILIFF

Reverend, you are greatly courageous and a great spirit, there is in you, at the same time, a soldier and a monk.

GRANDIER

There's a Christian, sir, and that's all.

BAILIFF

Well, it's agreed, I'll be on the look out for apparitions. I will watch for Returners and if they arise anew, I will come to find you and we will make the expedition together.

GRANDIER

It's a bargain, sir.

BAILIFF

Till we meet again, father, till we meet again.

(Exit Bailiff. Daniel appears.)

DANIEL

Ah—finally, he's gone. He's not bad. Is that bailiff a gossip?

GRANDIER

Daniel!

DANIEL

Yes, Daniel, Daniel, who has to come through the window because his brother shuts the door on him, and I think, God pardon me, after having shut the door on him, shuts his arms.

GRANDIER

Oh, no, no! Come, my child, come!

(He extends his arms, Daniel rushes to him. Urbain presses him to his heart, then breaks into tears, and sits on a chair while Daniel remains standing, enveloped in his arms.)

DANIEL

Poor brother, wouldn't it have been better to do this a long while ago? Today, perhaps the wound will scar.

GRANDIER

My dear child, it will without cease, and the wound will always bleed, only it will bleed inside, and no one will see it bleed, except God, who has taken Ursula from me, and you, who knew her.

DANIEL

Oh, I told mama, it was for this reason you wouldn't see us.

GRANDIER

I've been wrong. It would have been better to weep. When too many tears are stored up in the heart, they choke those who do not shed them. Oh, it's true, my child that God wants me to weep for her, right?

DANIEL

I weep for her a lot—I who she didn't love the way she loved you, I, who she only loved as a child and like a brother. So, you flee from yourself, whereas I remain.

GRANDIER

Would you want me after having just given myself entirely to God to offer the spectacle of my sorrow to men? Oh! It's the last feeling of pride which drags me—and indeed I am well punished for it, for I don't even know where she sleeps her last sleep—for through the tears I shed for her death I cannot even see her tomb.

DANIEL

She is in the de Sable cemetery, Brother and they've planted large trees on her tomb that can be seen from the fountain on the highway.

GRANDIER

And what is the shape of her sepulcher? Has she, at least, the flowers that she loved? They were white roses, jasmine, violets. Who takes care of all this? Who watches over the death of she who watched over the life of all?

DANIEL

Alas, I don't know how to tell you any more, brother, I have indeed like the others, gone from the church to the cemetery, but reaching the gate, thinking they were going to shut her in a somber cave or put her in a moist ditch, thinking I was going to hear screeching of the rusty hinges of a sepulchral gate, or the echo on the bier that first clump of earth which separates life from eternity, oh! Oh! I cried so much brother that my mother said to me, "Let's not go much further, my child," and then she led me away for she was weeping as much as I was, poor mother, go!

GRANDIER

And you never returned alone? And you never returned by yourself?

DANIEL

To the de Sable cemetery? No, never, never!

GRANDIER

Oh, I must know where she reposes, I must know her tomb. We are going to go there together, right my dear Daniel?

DANIEL

Where's that?

GRANDIER

To the de Sable cemetery.

(taking his hands and looking at him)

DANIEL

Oh, with you I will go wherever you wish, brother.

GRANDIER

Come, there.

DANIEL

(shutting his eyes)

Ah!

GRANDIER

Are you there?

DANIEL

Yes, wait—I think we are at the gate, but I cannot see very clearly.

(Grandier passes his hands before the child's eyes: his eyes open.)

GRANDIER

Do you see better?

DANIEL

Yes.

GRANDIER

Then lead me.

DANIEL

Ah—how sad it is, the cemetery, all the leaves are falling from the trees, like souls stealing away—all the flowers fading like dying candles.

GRANDIER

Ursula! Ursula!

DANIEL

Take care, brother! They say to strike the stone of a tomb brings bad luck. Take care and follow this little guide. It's down there, you see—by those four cypresses. Why didn't they plant other trees, not cypresses? Birds never rest in cypresses—and she, she loved the singing of birds.

GRANDIER

Ursula! Ursula!

DANIEL

We are there! Heavens, it's below this balustrade. There are four tombs in this little enclosure. That's not her—that's her mother. That's not her either—that's her brother—who was the same age as me, you know? And they called him Didier. Hello Didier—ah, ah, here's hers.

GRANDIER

Ursula! Ursula!

DANIEL

It's a great marble slab with a sculpted cross. Wait, I am going to read the inscription on the tomb. "Here rests the very highborn and very powerful Miss Ursula de Sable, Countess de Rovère. Born May 1, 1610, and returned to God, June 15, 1629.

GRANDIER

Holy Virgin, pray for me!

DANIEL

Oh—brother, oh! How strange this is?

GRANDIER

What?

DANIEL

I see under the stone as if there were no stone. I see in the vault as if it were lit.

GRANDIER

Well?

DANIEL

Well, there's a bier, but it is empty.

GRANDIER

What are you saying?

DANIEL

I say, I say, I say—there is no cadaver in the coffin.

GRANDIER

My God!

DANIEL

(looking around)

No! No! No!

GRANDIER

Why, then they must have removed her to put her in another sepulcher.

DANIEL

Wait, yes, I see them. It's a woman and two men. They are taking the cadaver and they're carrying it away.

GRANDIER

Where is this?

DANIEL

I am following them. Rest easy. They are putting her in a carriage. The carriage is leaving. She's entering Loudon. They are taking her out of the Convent of the Ursulines. It's at night. The woman has a key to the gate. She's opening it. She's indicating the cellars of the convent. Ah, now we are in the midst of tombs again. She's placing Ursula in a vault shut with a grill. She's lighting a lamp. She's putting bread and water near the body. She's leaving. Wait! Wait! My God! Ursula is waking up, it seems to me—yes, I see her—she's on her knees, she's praying—she's not dead!

GRANDIER

Ursula isn't dead?

DANIEL

Why, no—since I tell you she's praying—since I tell you I see her.

GRANDIER

Oh! You are sure? You are sure?

DANIEL

I see her.

GRANDIER

And can you lead me to her?

DANIEL

Yes, yes, certainly, if you don't wake me up.

GRANDIER

Ah! Come! Come!

DANIEL

Follow me!

(They leave.)

CURTAIN

ACT I

Scene 6

The sepulchral vault of the convent of the Ursulines. A large stairway. In the foreground an in-pace, isolated by a grill. The in-pace is to the spectator's left. A lamp lights it as with a strange daylight.

(Ursula is seated on straw. Before her Jeanne de Laubardemont, leaving the gate of the in pace.)

URSULA

But, still madam, you ought to have pity on me some day and tell me what crime I have committed to live here enchained in a dungeon in the center of the earth? And for how long I don't know, for I've stopped counting days and nights which are confused in an eternal obscurity for me.

JEANNE

Aren't you dead and resting in the place of the dead—isn't it the tomb?

URSULA

Oh! The dead—the dead at least sleep while waiting for the eternal resurrection, while for me deliverance—is death, is death!

JEANNE

Why wait for the death you implore? Why not go before it? Haven't you there, within your reach that which will rid you of life when life becomes a burden for you.

URSULA

Poison, isn't it? Why, instead of the narcotic they gave me, and which made me pass for dead, tell me why didn't they give me poison which would kill me right off?

JEANNE

Because she who wishes to avenge herself on you has no desire to commit a useless crime. Why kill you when she can let you live? In reality, aren't you dead? And do you think a real tomb can be any more deep and heavy than this prison which encloses you?

URSULA

I've understood only one word of what you've told me. That person who wishes to be avenged on me. That person is you, isn't it madam?

JEANNE

It is I—you said it.

URSULA

You avenge yourself on me! But in what way have I offended you? I never saw you before the day I awoke in this dungeon. I do not know you, and even today as you tell me that you are avenging yourself on me, I don't even know your name. no, madam, I repeat, you cannot avenge yourself on me—since I've never done you any injury.

JEANNE

You've never done me any injury? Look at me—I am still young, still beautiful, rich and of high birth—nothing forced me to take vows—and yet I wear this habit—I am superior of a convent, and once a day I am condemned to descend to the depths of this vault to bring you light and food. Well, these vows, this habit, even this crime that I am committing by separating you from the world—it's all your fault.

URSULA

If that is so, I ask your pardon—and I will pray for you, but I repeat, I don't understand.

JEANNE

You don't understand! So you think the only injury one woman can do to another is in poison she pours her, or in a dagger blow she's truck her? To give you an idea of injury, you must see the drink which poisons or the iron which kills! And the jealousy that a rival must drink, and the love disdained with which she tears your heart. That you count as nothing. You haven't injured me? Well, what does it matter to me if the injury doesn't come from you if it comes to me through you?

URSULA

Ah, you knew Urbain. You loved him. I understand completely. If you knew him, where is he, madam? What's he doing? What's become of him?

JEANNE

What does it matter to you where he is, what he's doing, what's become of him, since you are separated from him forever?

URSULA

That is the sentence you have pronounced, Madam. But it's not yet ratified by the Lord. The Lord is good. The Lord is merciful, as deeply as you have buried me, his glance will fall on me, or my prayer will rise to him. One day He will deliver me.

JEANNE

Has He delivered you in the last two years?

URSULA

Perhaps I am condemned as a test and I have not yet suffered enough.

JEANNE

Dream of events which can get you out of here—and tell me the ones you can rely on, let's see.

URSULA

Here, come closer and look at this drop of water, which falls every minute from the vault into this stone, and with such regularity that it helped me to tell the time—well, it's beginning to pierce the stone.

JEANNE

Perhaps it's fallen this way for a thousand years every minute.

URSULA

Well, I shall apply my spirit to my chain—I am young—I was nineteen years old when I was shut in here—and perhaps if only with my tears, I shall wear it out like this drop of water has done to the stone—and then—

JEANNE

And then you will find this grill shut, this door shut—will you wear them out with your tears?

URSULA

Well, he too is suffering—he too will look for me—for his part.

JEANNE

First of all, he thinks you are dead—and then, you know he's living, who told you he still loves you?

URSULA

Since you have taken vows, since you have taken the veil, since you descend to this dungeon once a day, you see quite clearly he hasn't stopped loving me.

JEANNE

So be it, suppose all that, Ursula, suppose your tears break your chain, suppose that Grandier still loves you, suppose that Grandier is searching for you, suppose he takes from me this key, which never leaves me, suppose you hear his step, suppose you hear his voice, suppose suddenly he appears through these bars—

URSULA

Oh, then, that day will repay me for all my troubles!

JEANNE

That day will be the most cruel and desperate of all your days, for in seeing him again, Ursula, the first sight of him will lose him to you forever.

URSULA

What do you mean?

JEANNE

Yes, Urbain still thinks of you, yes Urbain still loves you, he loves you more than you can imagine, more than you could dream, poor Urbain loves you, he loves you so much he's become a priest.

(She leaves.)

URSULA

(collapsing)

Oh! My God! My God! It's I who live and it's he who is dead! Poor Urbain, he loved me so much that he renounced this world the moment they told him I was no more? Oh! The Lord is my witness, Urbain, that in my most desperate, mortal hours, I never for a moment doubted your love. Urbain, you were there eternally near me, and I saw you, I heard you, and I said to myself, Oh, he must think I am dead since he hasn't yet found me." Oh, if I had a way to let him know that I am living, if I had a way to let him know where I am! My God, my God, advise me, inspire me, my God!

(Grandier appears at the rear as Ursula prays. Suddenly Ursula shivers.)

URSULA

Oh! What is this? I am so accustomed to the silence of this solitude, my ear knows all the noise of the water in the depths of these rocks, the noise of the wind under the vaults. That is neither the murmur of the water, nor the wailing of the wind—it's the steps of two persons—yes? Why two people? This woman always comes alone—anyway, she left. Why would she return? My God! Pardon me, but it seems to be his step, it seems it is his step and that of Daniel—oh, my heart, don't beat so hard, you will prevent me from hearing.

(Ursula [in the in-pace] Grandier and Daniel are on the other side of the bars.)

DANIEL

Come, my brother—we are getting close.

GRANDIER

Getting close you say?

DANIEL

Yes - heavens, there.

(pointing his finger)

URSULA

Oh, my God! My God!

GRANDIER

But there's a grill which prevents us from reaching her.

URSULA

It's his voice! That's his voice!

DANIEL

Wait.

GRANDIER

What are you doing?

DANIEL

Wait, I tell you.

(touching the bars of the grill one after the other)

Pull this bar, brother, its eaten away with rust; it will give way.

GRANDIER

This one?

DANIEL

Yes.

GRANDIER

My God, give me the strength.

URSULA

It's him! It's Urbain.

(trying to break her chain)

Urbain, it's Ursula! Urbain, help me, help me, I am here.

GRANDIER

(pushing the bar)

Wait! Wait! Here I am!

(With a violent effort, Ursula breaks her chain and meanwhile, Grandier forces the bars; they rush into each others arms. Daniel sits motionless.)

GRANDIER and DANIEL

Ursula!

URSULA

Grandier! Ah, I knew indeed you would find me.

GRANDIER

(looking at his robe)

My God, my God, in seeing her again I've forgotten everything—Ursula, pardon me.

URSULA

(falling to her knees)

Your blessing, father.

GRANDIER

Oh, yes, be blessed, angel from heaven, who, for me, has suffered like a martyr! Be blessed, you who god forbids me to love like a lover—but permits me to love like a sister.

URSULA

Alas! Alas!

GRANDIER

Ursula, my sister, have pity on me, help my courage instead of weakening it. Ursula, the important thing, first of all to get you out of here. Where is the key to this grill?

URSULA

The woman who holds me prisoner wears it eternally above her neck and you cannot take it from her.

GRANDIER

Perhaps.

(calling)

Daniel!

DANIEL

(rising and coming)

Here I am.

URSULA

My God, what's wrong with him. I don't recognize either, his voice or his bearing—you'd say he's dead.

GRANDIER

Don't be uneasy. Ursula. Daniel, the woman who was here just now, the woman who holds Ursula shut up here—is she the same woman you saw opening the tomb?

DANIEL

Yes—she's the same one.

GRANDIER

Do you know her?

DANIEL

Yes, I know her.

GRANDIER

What's her name?

DANIEL

Jeanne de Laubardemont!

GRANDIER

I suspected that. Does the key to this grill sometimes leave her?

DANIEL

Never!

GRANDIER

Where does she wear it?

DANIEL

Ursula told you—around her neck.

GRANDIER

Is there a way to get it from her?

DANIEL

The one you are thinking of.

GRANDIER

You think I will succeed?

DANIEL

With God's help—yes!

GRANDIER

Where can I find her at this moment?

DANIEL

In the cloister where she's giving a party for her nuns.

GRANDIER

Which way will get me there?

DANIEL

This way leads there.

GRANDIER

Ursula, in a half hour, you will be free or I will be dead.

URSULA

Lord, Lord, what is happening? Is what I see with my eyes truly real?

DANIEL

Fear nothing, sister—God is with him.

(Grandier goes back through the opening and rapidly disappears while signaling to Ursula that he's going to return. Ursula follows him avidly with her eyes—her hand passing between the bars of the grill.)

BLACKOUT

ACT I

Scene 7

The Cloister of the Ursuline Convent. The foreground is lit, through the arcades can be seen the cypresses in the lit up gardens. The cloister, at the left is plunged in infinite darkness.

At the rise of the curtain, two nuns, dressed in white, covered by veils cross the stage. Nogaret enters and notices two nuns dressed in worldly costume. He gestures to Barace who approaches—each of them takes the arm of a nun.

Jeanne de Laubardemont enters in her turn. The Lords straighten up and arrange themselves at her approach. She sits on a tomb, then they bring her an ancient type harp.

The ballet is danced.

The last step is danced by two Spaniards. It's a very fast bolero. At the moment when the lips of the two women touch, a change in the music signals the apparition of Grandier. Everyone flees. Jeanne wants to flee, too, but stays rooted to the steps of the tomb. Urbain approaches her with an imperious gesture. She takes the key from her neck and gives it to Urbain who slowly vanishes. Jeanne remains motionless.

CURTAIN

ACT II

Scene 8

Urbain's cell.

(Grandier enters with Ursula hidden under the robe of a monk.)

GRANDIER

(from the door)

Come in, Ursula, Daniel, go find my mother without telling her the reason and bring her here. Come in, Ursula.

URSULA

(sitting)

Oh—I cannot believe in your presence nor in my freedom. It seems to me that what has just happened is a sweet and beautiful dream which will vanish on waking up.

GRANDIER

Thank God, Ursula! For your deliverance is—if not a dream, at least a miracle; it was God who revealed to me your existence hidden from the rest of the world, it was God who led me to your dungeon and I still hope it is God who permits me to bring you here.

(Going to the Madonna and drawing the curtains.)

URSULA

What are you doing, Urbain?

GRANDIER

Nothing.

URSULA

Yes, you're right, it's God who permits you to bring me here, for here, like down there, I will be dead to the rest of the world, but living for heaven and for you.

GRANDIER

Beware, Ursula, beware of letting yourself regain a hope which cannot be realized.

URSULA

What?

GRANDIER

What I think, I read through your words, what this habit you've just put on gives rise to, that your entry to this cell has confirmed.

URSULA

Urbain, my friend, hardly reunited, is it your intention to separate us?

GRANDIER

Ursula, the longer we wait, the greater the sorrow will be.

URSULA

But do you think this woman can reclaim me, pursue me?

GRANDIER

No, I don't think so, and in all probability she will keep silent, about what she has done and what I have seen.

URSULA

Can't you have me received as a novice, Urbain?—can't I, hidden under this costume, escape the notice of the community?

GRANDIER

All that is possible, Ursula, yes, you can live here hidden from all eyes, and the solitude of the cloister is so profound, that you can leave earth and return to heaven without the earth suspecting you've been gone for an instant.

URSULA

Well, then?

GRANDIER

But where the eyes of man do not reach, God's glance penetrates. In the depths of this cell, under that dress, however, well you hide yourself, God will see you, Ursula.

URSULA

Well, what will he see, Urbain? Two pure and loving beings who will sing his praise in the profound gratitude of their hearts, who melt together their souls in the same prayers, eternal prayers that the first will have begun, and that the second will finish, who have no other desire than to become more pure through each other, to leave on earth, what belongs to earth, and each instant will see the creation of a feather in the wings which one day will carry us to God.

GRANDIER

Yes, Ursula, you see things this way, because you are an angel, because your feet hardly touch the dirt of the world. Never having failed, you think you are infallible, but I—I who love you more than my will, beyond my strength, I feel that my soul will let itself be consumed by the flames of my body—oh, I tell you, we must separate.

URSULA

Urbain, Urbain, if you insist that I leave you after having lost me and found me again so—it's because you do not love me.

GRANDIER

I don't love you—I who ruined you for having loved you too much! Oh, my God, you who, for two years, heard my cries, saw my tears, counted my lamentations, O, my God, my God, you who, I hope, will forgive me for this wild love—you hear her. She tells me I don't love her.

URSULA

(rising)

Well, so be it! I will separate myself from you, Urbain—I will leave the Convent, I will stay in the town, but no longer able to speak to you, I will see you, and hear you at least, I will hear you when at church you speak of charity, of religion, of love, of another existence where the souls of those who have suffered and have been separated in this world will be reunited and happy. I will see you when you pass bearing alms for the poor, consolation to the rich, prayer to the dying and always, you will belong to me as I want to see you from now on like a celestial intermediary between men and God.

GRANDIER

Yes, you will see me that way, but I, I have neither your eyes nor your heart. I will see with you as a woman in this church where I owe my whole being to the Lord. I will belong only to you. If they call on me, as you said, to bring alms to the poor, consolation to the sick, prayer to the dying instead of going straight to my sacred end. I will deviate from my way to pass by where you will be. And when I arrive, regretting leaving you, forgetting the Creator for his creation. I will arrive too late, the poor will be hungry and cold. The sick will have suffered and the dying will have died. And there are many voices, which will accuse me before God, and these voices will be so numerous, so that on the day of judgment, the Lord will separate me, I, guilty of every sin, from you, guilty of none.

URSULA

Oh, my God! My God!

GRANDIER

No, my Ursula no, let's not tempt God! Return to Sable, to your Château, near the charming village of Rovère, where my mother and my brother will be living. You know my cell, I know your Château—you will see me in the midst of my books, of my musical instruments and chemistry, dividing my hours between prayer and work, and thinking of you while I work and pray. I will see you between your birds and your flowers, your birds which brighten up the air, and your flowers which perfume it—I will say to myself, "She is sad because I am far from her. She dreams because she's thinking of me." There, you see, Ursula, I am the eldest, and I ought to die first, a first death. God, which forbids you from my cell—commands you to my tomb. I shall ask to share the sepulcher of my fathers. They will take me back to Rome, my mother will no longer be—my brother is a child, he'll run around the world and will have forgotten me. I will have no one except you. You will be my only love in death as you have been in life. My death, Ursula, will almost reunite us. Your death will reunite us completely.

URSULA

Let it be according to your will and not according to mine, Urbain.

GRANDIER

Daniel and my mother are entering the convent, Ursula. I am going to tell them everything or rather tell everything to my mother.

URSULA

Do you think Daniel hasn't told her everything?

GRANDIER

Daniel knows nothing, Ursula, Daniel cannot tell her anything.

URSULA

But didn't he see me and didn't he hear me? Wasn't it he who led you to me?

GRANDIER

Yes, but he was asleep when he did that and on his awakening, he will forget it.

URSULA

I don't understand.

GRANDIER

Go into that closet, Ursula. They are coming.

URSULA

It seems to me, if I was in your place, having so little time to ourselves, I wouldn't want to be separated from you for a minute.

GRANDIER

Will you be separated from me by this tapestry through which you can hear everything, and almost see as well?

URSULA

(making a gesture to throw herself in his arms)

Yes, Grandier! You are right to insist that I leave you.

(She leaves.)

DANIEL

(out of breath)

Ah, there you are.

GRANDIER

And my mother?

DANIEL

Poor woman! You can't be mad at her. She's coming with her fifty year old legs and I'm coming on my sixteen-year old legs and heavens, you see, she's not very late, poor mother. Good mother, come, come! Here he is, your son—

(looking around him)

Heavens, where is the little monk?

GRANDIER

Mother?

MME. GRANDIER

(entering)

Grandier! Grandier—I am not angry with you for having been together without seeing me. I've been young. I've loved and I understand.

GRANDIER

Oh saintly woman, who begins by pardoning him. Thanks! Oh, I am going to give you back, I hope, some of the joy I've taken from you.

MME. GRANDIER

What do you mean?

GRANDIER

Daniel! Watch that no one disturbs us.

DANIEL

(low)

Brother, where is the little monk who was with you when you woke me up, and who shook my hand, it seems to me, when you told me to go find our mother?

GRANDIER

You will see him again soon, go, child, go.

DANIEL

Will I have to be on guard a long while?

GRANDIER

No, don't worry.

DANIEL

Good.

(he leaves)

MME. GRANDIER

Do you like it better here than your room in de Rovère?

GRANDIER

Mother, I came here to find two things that can be found, no where else; solitude and silence. In silence God speaks to the heart of man; in solitude man speaks to the heart of God.

MME. GRANDIER

When you spoke to God, did God answer to you?

GRANDIER

Yes, mother.

MME. GRANDIER

And what did you ask?

GRANDIER

Peace for me, happiness for you.

MME. GRANDIER

And he gave you peace?

GRANDIER

He gave me all I asked of him, mother.

MME. GRANDIER

Thanks to God, then! If you are happy, Grandier, what does the rest matter?

GRANDIER

I told you, mother, that God granted me peace, and I hope that at this same time, he gave you happiness.

MME. GRANDIER

(shaking her head)

I had two children, Grandier.

GRANDIER

Well, if in the place of a son that he took from you, he gave you back a daughter?

MME. GRANDIER

Alas, I had a daughter, also and she is dead!

GRANDIER

Mother, do you recall that sacred story of the daughter of Jaire, which you often told me when I was a child. They thought her dead, right? Her father himself after having bathed her in perfumes, buried her in the tomb. Jesus passed by, he saw the tears of those who loved her, he touched her with the tip of his finger and the daughter of Jaire extended her arms to her father, saying, "You called me, father, here I am."

MME. GRANDIER

Yes, but it was only two days that the daughter of Jaire slept in her tomb and it's been two years that the one we weep for was buried in hers.

GRANDIER

Mother, you don't doubt in the complete power of God, do you?

MME. GRANDIER

What do you mean, Grandier? Are you speaking of Ursula de Sable?

GRANDIER

Yes, mother.

MME. GRANDIER

Do you mean we are deceived? Do you mean Ursula didn't die?

GRANDIER

Yes, mother.

MME. GRANDIER

Oh! Impossible! Didn't you see her on her funeral bed, didn't I follow her coffin as far as the cemetery, wasn't she buried in the tomb with her ancestors?

GRANDIER

Yes, mother.

MME. GRANDIER

Well—what are you saying then?

GRANDIER

That God is great and that he brought the daughter of Jaire back to life.

MME. GRANDIER

Ursula! Ursula!

URSULA

You called me, mother, and here I am!

MME. GRANDIER

Miss de Sable.

URSULA

Oh, I called you mother!

MME. GRANDIER

My daughter.

GRANDIER

(on his knees—arms to heaven)

My God, you have blessed me in spite of my deserts.

DANIEL

(entering)

Brother! Brother! Guards—clerks—they are looking for you. They demand you.

GRANDIER

They demand me? They are looking for me? And who is that?

MIGNON

(entering with guards and clerks)

I! Here's the guilty man, gentleman.

GRANDIER

The guilty man.

MIGNON

Do your duty.

A CLERK

In the name of the King, I arrest you!

MME. GRANDIER, DANIEL, and URSULA

They are arresting him! Him! In the name of the king?

GRANDIER

Gentlemen, you know, I belong to a religious order, and I only answer to ecclesiastical justice.

MIGNON

(to the Clerk)

Read your mandate, sir.

A CLERK

(reading)

"Henry-Louis Chataignier de la Roche-Pozay by divine grace, Bishop of Poitiers, seeing the charges and information given by the archbishop of Loudon, has ordered and orders, that Urbain Grandier, accused of disobedience and sacrilege by the opposition he made to the taking of the veil by Bianca dei Albizzio, be led and taken to the prison of the city, by the first Beadle, priest or tonsured clerk, and abandon him to the first royal sergeant to whom we give power to fulfill this mandate notwithstanding opposition or appeal whatever. Given at Dessai—the 22nd day of October 1637—signed Henry Louis, Bishop of Poitiers."

GRANDIER

There is nothing to say, gentlemen. The order is quite legal.

A CLERK

Then you make no opposition?

GRANDIER

None.

URSULA

My God!

MME. GRANDIER

My son!

DANIEL

My brother!

(throwing himself in Urbain's arms)

URSULA

Grandier!

OFFICER

(to scribe)

Sit and write.

GRANDIER

Don't worry, mother, don't worry, Daniel.

A CLERK

(dictating)

"On the 2nd day of October 1637, the day following the one on which this mandate was issued, we, Louis Chauvet, royal sergeant came to the cell of the aforesaid and have proceeded to arrest him in the presence of three persons found in his cell—the first, of these person being"—

(Madame Grandier)

Your full name and relationship, Madam.

MME. GRANDIER

Marie-Estève Grandier—his mother, sir.

A CLERK

(repeating)

Marie-Estève Grandier, his mother.

The second—

(to Daniel)

Who are you and what is your name?

DANIEL

Daniel Grandier, his brother.

A CLERK

(repeating)

Daniel Grandier, his brother—and the third—

(to Ursula)

Come here!

(Ursula remains motionless)

Come here, now!

GRANDIER

Tell him boldly who you are.

(pushing her forward)

ALL

Ursula!

MIGNON

A woman!

A CLERK

Come forward and give your name.

URSULA

I am Ursula de Sable, Countess de Rovère. When Urbain Grandier was living in the world, I was the fiancée of Urbain Grandier.

ALL

A woman.

MIGNON

A woman! A woman in the habit of a monk, a woman hidden in the cell as a monk—record this fact, sir, say, say that at the moment you came to arrest this wretch, a woman was hidden in his cell.

GRANDIER

(to Mignon)

Take care, brother! You are giving yourself up to rage—and rage is one of the seven deadly sins.

MIGNON

(to the Clerk)

Write! Write!

A CLERK

Don't worry, sir—all these things will be revealed at the trial.

URSULA

But, gentlemen, I've hardly been here an hour. Why this habit—I've only worn it since this evening.

MME. GRANDIER

Gentlemen.

DANIEL

Gentlemen.

MIGNON

Wait a minute! I recall coming once to this cell and having seen a portrait of the Virgin.

(looking at Ursula)

The resemblance—

(drawing the curtain)

Sacrilegious profanation! This pagan has given the Virgin a resemblance to his mistress.

GRANDIER

Why not as the Virgin who is at the side of God above is not more holy or more pure than the virgin who is at my side?

MIGNON

Write! Write! What are you doing—you aren't writing.

A CLERK

Sir, I've been ordered to arrest the Superior of the Convent, not to interrogate him. All that concerns the arrest is my affair—I've done my duty, the judge will do his. Take the accused to the prison of the city. We have nothing more to do here.

GRANDIER

Mother! Brother!

(He pulls them to his heart, but as to Ursula who opens her arms to him, he contents himself by pointing to heaven.)

I follow you, gentlemen

(He leaves.)

MONKS

(coming over to stare at Ursula)

A woman! A woman in our holy habit!

MIGNON

Say a demon, brothers! Ursula de Sable, Countess de Rovère has been dead and buried for two years.

BLACKOUT

ACT II

Scene 9

The Prison.

GRANDIER

(alone)

In prison—! Little matter what becomes of me—but her—her—what have they done—and to whom can I entrust her that has some power? Alas, if I, absent, she should fall back into the hands of her enemy! My mother, Daniel—an old woman and a child—they are her only protectors.

JAILOR

This way, sir, enter.

GRANDIER

(delighted)

The Bailiff. My God, it's you who sent him—you who are the true protector of the poor and oppressed—and I had forgotten.

JAILOR

(appearing first)

There—there he is!

BAILIFF

Leave me with him, I want to question him.

JAILOR

Oh, well, then you are going to have a long talk—it seems he's got a lot to answer for.

GRANDIER

(who has heard him)

To interrogate me! Well, I find an adversary where I thought to find a friend.

(the jailor leaves)

To interrogate me! You came to interrogate me, sir, do you say?

BAILIFF

(quite loud)

Yes, sir, and I hope you will reply fully to me.

(low)

Especially now that clown has gone.

GRANDIER

Oh—I wasn't mistaken—it's a friend who comes to me.

BAILIFF

(extending his two hands toward him)

Eh! Yes, my dear Grandier, it's a friend, but let's speak low, for, as your jailor said just now, you are not here for a little thing it seems.

GRANDIER

I am here for the action that you know and that you yourself approved of.

BAILIFF

What action?

GRANDIER

For my opposition to the orders of Cardinal Richelieu in poor Bianca dei Albizzio's taking the veil.

BAILIFF

Ta, ta, ta, ta! At the moment it is really a question of Bianca dei Albizzio.

GRANDIER

In that case, what is it a question of?

BAILIFF

Of matters which will get you burned ten times, and me once, my dear Grandier, if they knew I came to see you in your prison.

GRANDIER

Get me burned ten times! Why you are mad, Bailiff! What are these matters?

BAILIFF

Well—half the convent is possessed—You've put the devil in the bodies of all these saintly girls through a pact you've made with Satan. Mignon and his acolyte Barace have already interrogated two or three—why do I say interrogated? Exorcised, and the responses have been unanimous—as it seems—each one says the name of the devil she has had in her womb and the name of the magician who sent them there.

GRANDIER

Is it Guillaume Cerisay La Guerinière—Bailiff of Loudon is who speaks to me or is it still a child who is completely enchanted by the blue stories of his nurse?

BAILIFF

Yes, it is I who speak to you, and what I tell you is not madness—I repeat it to you.

GRANDIER

And these devils, sent by me into the bodies of nuns—do they know their names, at least?

BAILIFF

By God, the first thing they did in taking possession of the domicile was to name themselves. The one in Sister Louise des Anges is called Beherit, the one in Sister Catherine de la Presentation, Cerberus—the one of Sister Elizabeth of the Cross, Astorath.

GRANDIER

Do I have business with a serious man or a man speaking seriously?

BAILIFF

That man speaks to you with tears in his eyes and terror in his heart, my dear Grandier.

GRANDIER

And this magician, this enchanter who made the pact—it's me?

BAILIFF

By God! Who do you think it may be?

GRANDIER

But no one has dreamed such stupidity for three centuries.

BAILIFF

I ask your pardon, my dear friend—and the Parliament of Aix has just burned Gaufredi on similar accusations.

GRANDIER

(going to sit down)

Come on! People who know me won't believe it.

BAILIFF

You know the Latin axiom *"Credo quia absurdum"*—I believe because it is absurd—I know of nothing more profound and especially more true.

GRANDIER

You believe it—you?

BAILIFF

I don't say that I believe; I say—they believe.

GRANDIER

What does it matter to me what fools say! What does it matter to me what people of bad faith believe!

BAILIFF

It's the fools who will testify against you; it's the people of bad faith who will judge you.

GRANDIER

Well, so be it!

BAILIFF

What do you mean, so be it?

GRANDIER

Little matter what god decides about me, Master William, and very happy will be the day, by whatever means, his will takes me from this world—but—

BAILIFF

But what?

GRANDIER

But there is in all this, a woman, a young girl, an angel.

BAILIFF

Ah, yes, the woman in the picture, the woman in the monk's habit, the dead woman, right?

GRANDIER

There is an Ursula de Sable, sir, over whom, in the name of Heaven, in the name of your wife, in the name of your children, over whom I beg you to watch as you would watch over one of your daughters.

BAILIFF

Watch over her?

GRANDIER

Yes.

BAILIFF

Why where do you want me to take her from?

GRANDIER

From where she is, wherever they took her.

BAILIFF

Who knows, since she has disappeared?

GRANDIER

Ursula has disappeared? She must have fallen back into the hands of that woman.

BAILIFF

My dear Grandier, pardon me, but I think that, in regard to the habit that you wear, there are many too many women in this affair. Here we have, first of all, the Miss de Sable who was believed to be dead, who is living: Then we have Sister Elizabeth; then we have Sister Catherine, then we have Sister Louise—that everyone thought were saintly girls, and who are what? The devil incarnated nothing more than that—still, as if there weren't enough women in play, here's yet another woman, a woman unknown who has come to take a role in this tragedy, for it is a tragedy, I maintain, my dear Grandier, and the proof, the proof is that, if I have advice to give you, it's not to occupy yourself with such a woman but to think of yourself, of gaining your liberty and securing your safety.

GRANDIER

I would like to follow your advice, Bailiff, but, it seems to me, it would be a difficult thing. The corridors are very well guarded, and unless you sacrifice yourself for me, and you take my dress in exchange for your clothes.

BAILIFF

Not at all, no, no! My devotion doesn't go that far. The devil, they would burn me in your stead, and although sensitive to cold, my love for the fire stops at a certain distance from the pyre. I wish to save you, but I don't wish to ruin myself. I consent to compromise myself a little, but not much.

GRANDIER

For the little you have come, Bailiff, I am very grateful, be sure of it.

BAILIFF

I don't know if I've come for a little or for a lot, but I've come to tell you a secret that I think is known to me alone and which may be of some importance to you. Listen carefully. My grandfather was the architect of Loudon, it was he who built the prisons of the city. The thing happened at the beginning of the reign of Charles the IX. They put powerful Huguenots in these prisons, and it was all quite simple, since it was for this they had been built, but what was less simple is that they didn't always leave by the way they had entered.

GRANDIER

Yes, I understand—certain executions which weren't brought to registers of the tribunal were carried out in the dungeons.

BAILIFF

Exactly. They were in most of these prisons secret doors, unknown to the prisoners through which the executioners entered.

GRANDIER

They murdered them.

BAILIFF

Call it whatever you wish. I won't contradict you, Grandier,—only listen here, for it's important. As the Seneschal, who built the monument was a careful man, and the history of Enguerrand de Marigny, who was hanged on the gibbet he had raised often was recalled to his memory, he said to my father—"My dear Cerisay, today it's we who are imprisoning the Huguenots, well and good—but if luck turns and tomorrow it will be the Huguenots who imprison us in their turn, let us arrange things in that case, so that the secret door which serves for entrance can at the same time, function as an exit"— Then, everything was done in accordance with the desires of the good Seneschal. The door which opens from without, opens from within. The thing is to know the secret—thus, if you prefer, as I do, a good flight to a bad murder—

GRANDIER

Well?

BAILIFF

Well, probe the walls, my dear friend, look high, look low—push your finger into all rough spots—don't tire. Probably no one but you and I in the world knows the secret of these doors. My father died telling me and my faith, and doing as he did, I am telling you: you who have a great need, as it seems to me.

GRANDIER

And you think my cell possesses one of these doors?

BAILIFF

I can't answer to you for that, because I never answer for anything, but, it's a good bet. The Seneschal had the happy thought, to inspire pious ideas in the prisoners, by sculpting in the wall of each cell one of the instruments which played a role in the passion of Our Lord, such as the sponge, the whip, the nail, the lance, the dice, you are in the cell of the dice, why wouldn't it have its doors like the others?

GRANDIER

Thanks, Bailiff, but to flee would be to give advantage to the cause of my persecutors. I am innocent; I will await my judgment with tranquility.

BAILIFF

But if they condemn you?

GRANDIER

It's the martyrs who uphold the faith.

BAILIFF

That's fine, that's fine—be a martyr if it is your vocation, but it seems to me you had spoken of a young girl.

GRANDIER

Yes, Ursula de Sable.

BAILIFF

I don't ask you her name, I haven't the least desire to know it—only you said she had fallen back into the hands of a certain woman—

GRANDIER

Well?

BAILIFF

Well, if only to get her out of those clutches, I would look for this secret.

GRANDIER

Oh! Yes, you are right, Bailiff. Right now even—

(looking around him)

Happily, this lamp.

BAILIFF

Plague! Let me leave before finding the secret and especially before using it. If, when returning, the jailor found me alone, he could very well, for greater security, shut me up in another cell and who can say if it would have two doors?

GRANDIER

Yes, dear Bailiff, go.

BAILIFF

Wait a while—what the devil. Before you were in no great rush, and now here you are in a big hurry. I don't wish to do things by half. Who says that you are able to get out of here? May God wish it—who says, you won't encounter some resistance? You were a soldier before becoming a monk—have you some weapon?

GRANDIER

None: The weapon of the innocent—is his innocence.

BAILIFF

Yes, it's a defensive weapon, moreover, I believe, seeing the gravity of the situation that an offensive weapon.--

(looking around him)

Take my sword.

GRANDIER

Thanks, thanks, Bailiff, but if something goes wrong—and it is recognized—

BAILIFF

That would be a difficult thing. I have, for this use, taken it from an armory where it's been shut up for perhaps the last 30 years—which doesn't prevent it being useful and properly sharpened. In any case, if you have occasion of using it—which God forbid—as two precautions are better than one—if after using it, you pass by a river, let it fall in the river. I don't expect you to return it to me.

GRANDIER

Oh, my friend, my only friend!

BAILIFF

Hush! And hide this sword somewhere for me—I keep the sheath, you understand, to raise my mantle, in seeing me with a scabbard at my side, they won't suspect that the blade remains with you. You will hide it under your mattress. Only you must be careful when the jailor comes to make your bed. Happily, he won't often give himself that trouble! Goodbye now—

(low)

And may the Lord protect you!

GRANDIER

Goodbye! Goodbye!

BAILIFF

Say goodbye to me, like a man in a bad humor says goodbye.

(going to the door and rapping)

Hey, jailor, hey!

JAILOR

(from the end of the corridor)

Wait, Mr. Bailiff, wait.

GRANDIER

By the way, what time is it?

BAILIFF

Oh—at least ten o'clock. I suspect that at present no one will come to bother you, you have the whole night before you, and in October, the nights are lengthy. Hush!

JAILOR

Here I am, Mr. Bailiff. Here I am.

(Low regarding Grandier, who is sitting on his bed)

Well, what do you think about it?

BAILIFF

Hum! Hum!

JAILOR

What! Is it as serious at that?

BAILIFF

Hum!

JAILOR

Ah—the devil!

(They leave.)

GRANDIER

(watching and listening to them go)

Yes, yes, the Bailiff is right. First of all, let's save Ursula. Oh, when I'm alone, when I have nothing to fear except for myself, I will be strong. God doesn't wish a Christian to attack, but he allows man to defend himself. But first of all, Ursula, above all—let's see how you save her—this dungeon must have a secret door—and supposing that it has one, it is in stone like the rest, and only a long search will discover it. Ah, I will have patience. I will search till I discover it.

(listening)

What's that? A noise of steps again. They're coming to my dungeon, they're stopping at the door—I hear the key turn in the lock—

(blowing out his lamp and hiding the sword)

Who is coming here?

JEANNE

You've read the order?

JAILOR

Yes, Madam.

JEANNE

Leave me alone with the prisoner—only at my first cry, at my first call, run—it could happen that I may need help. Go.

(The jailor leaves.)

GRANDIER

Who is this woman?

(approaching)

Jeanne!

JEANNE

Yes, Jeanne de Laubardemont.

GRANDIER

What have you come here for, Madam?

JEANNE

I am come to propose a treaty to you, Grandier.

GRANDIER

You know there is no pact possible between you and me. A pact is possible only between accomplices.

JEANNE

Peace then. We are enemies and enemies make peace.

GRANDIER

Before any peace is possible between us, I must be told who this unknown woman is who came to carry off during the night, the living dead girl from the tomb of her ancestors in order to shut her in the tomb I took her from.

JEANNE

It was I.

GRANDIER

I must be told further, who is the accuser who, forestalling the accusation I could bring had me arrested this morning under the pretext of disobedience to the orders of Cardinal Richelieu.

JEANNE

It was I.

GRANDIER

You confess them?

JEANNE

Why not? You are alone, and to your eyes, I don't wish to appear other than I am.

GRANDIER

And what feelings can motivate such actions? Speak.

JEANNE

Two opposing sentiments, and which have the very same source. I love you and I hate her.

GRANDIER

Take care, Madam. Love and hate are bad councilors.

JEANNE

You think so?

GRANDIER

Two furious demons which are leading you to the abyss.

JEANNE

(sitting down)

Explain that to me, Grandier.

GRANDIER

Yes, so long as you hold me shut in this dungeon—there must finally come a day of public interrogation.

JEANNE

Tomorrow—you will be publicly interrogated in the church of Saint Pierre.

GRANDIER

Then, tell me, aren't you afraid of what I will say?

JEANNE

What will you say—? Let's see!

GRANDIER

I will say that at the risk of poisoning her you applied a narcotic to a woman; I will say you removed her from her tomb, only to shut her in a prison worse than the tomb. I will say further, that by a miracle of God. I removed her from that prison, where, without me, she was going to die of cold, of misery and despair. That's what I will say.

JEANNE

As for me, I will reply that, as you are a man of the people, Grandier, and as Ursula de Sable was a daughter of the nobility, you gave her, not a narcotic to make her sleep but a potion to make her love you. I will reply that, during her sleep, you made her pass for dead, that you in fact buried her in a tomb as you buried yourself in a monastery—but that all this was simulated, the death of the mistress and the vows of the lover. I will reply that you took her from this tomb at night to bring her to your convent, that you made sacrilegious disguise from a monk's habit, of a cell for prayer, a boudoir for debauchery, and I will add that the proof of what I say is that the Clerk who came to arrest you for resistance to the orders of the Cardinal, found this Ursula de Sable that everyone thought dead—in your cell concealed in the garments of a monk.

GRANDIER

Ah, but you are forgetting that this weapon which you use against me, I can turn against you. You forget the nights of feasting and orgies, safeguarded by the rumors of ghosts. You forget that yesterday I surprised you, you and your nuns, dressed in worldly clothes; the daughters of the Lord were giving—in a cloister, by starlight a ball—to elegant and mysterious cavaliers—you are still forgetting that you didn't have strength remaining except to give me, on my order, this precious key which opened the dungeon of your prisoner—for you remained motionless, changed to a statue, when you saw me—the man of God, wandering in the midst of the nocturnal infamy.

JEANNE

What does what you just said prove? That Grandier is a clever magician, as witness the instruments of alchemy and books on the Cabala found in his cell. Because Grandier has made a pact with Satan, and thanks to this pact, the hearts of the most saintly belong to him, the souls of the most pure—submit to him—because, one day, tired of having only one mistress, like the King, he needed an entire harem like a sultan. You see, Grandier, far from denying it, we will confess—only our confessions will be mortal accusations against your life and your honor.

GRANDIER

Then I will pray God to enlighten my judge, God who has already made a miracle in my favor—won't abandon me part way on the path.

JEANNE

Again, you are mistaken, Grandier. God won't make a new miracle in your favor—God will not enlighten your judge—for your judge—your judge will be Jacques de Laubardemont.

GRANDIER

Your father?

JEANNE

My father!

GRANDIER

Oh, if that's the way it is.

JEANNE

Well?

GRANDIER

Beware!

JEANNE

Of what?

GRANDIER

I tell you, beware—understand? For God may indeed have sent me the judge—that the judge be judged.

JEANNE

(rising)

You are senseless, Grandier.

GRANDIER

(returning to her)

That's true!

JEANNE

Ah! You admit you are vanquished.

GRANDIER

Yes.

JEANNE

Do you want peace, Grandier?

GRANDIER

On what condition?

JEANNE

Grandier, I love you.

GRANDIER

In taking this habit, I said goodbye to all lovers.

JEANNE

Except your love for Ursula.

GRANDIER

That love was in me, and has transformed itself with me; earthly passion has become divine love; I love Ursula as I love my sister, as I love my mother, as I love the Holy Virgin that I have adored for two years under Ursula's features. If Ursula is free, if Ursula is safe, then let them put a world between Ursula and me. I consent to it, if there is no space for spirits, there is no distance between souls.

JEANNE

A thing is going to astonish you, Grandier—it's that I believe you. For I've had this confession even from the mouth of Ursula. Ursula wanted to live near you, and it was you who separated her, but if you separated her, if you had this control over yourself, it's because you love her, isn't it? It's that you are afraid of falling, isn't it? Well, I, whom you hate, near me you will be sure of living strong, I who you refuse to take in love—take me in pity. Listen, for a woman everything depends, from the first step she takes in life, if she's mistaken, the error drives her to misfortune, misfortune to despair, despair to crime, crime to impiety. Grandier, before you've seen me unhappy, after that you saw me desperate, today you see me criminal. Tomorrow—God knows that I will be tomorrow.

Grandier, stop me before I arrive at the summit of a horrible mountain. Grandier, stop me before I hurl myself. Yes, I recognize your word is holy and comes from God. Grandier, don't refuse to me because I love you what you would grant to the last woman who would come to the altar of penitence to demand: your support. See, Grandier, see what triumph, if you lead this straying soul back to God, if of a hardened criminal you make a submissive lamb. Peace, Grandier, peace.

GRANDIER

Well, yes, peace, Madam, but on one condition, Madam.

JEANNE

What is it?

GRANDIER

It's that the same city not contain us both, either I leave Loudon or you do.

JEANNE

Oh! No, no, no, Grandier! Grandier I want to see you—I need to see you. I cannot live without seeing you.

GRANDIER

Oh! Jeanne! Jeanne! You see clearly that—

JEANNE

What?

GRANDIER

You don't wish for me to save you—you want me to damn myself with you.

JEANNE

Well, yes—hell—but with you, Grandier, you are right, it's not peace that I offer you—it's your love I want.

GRANDIER

I took an oath on the altar.

JEANNE

You repulse me? Take care, Urbain! I have a hostage, a cherished hostage, an adored hostage—Ursula is in my hands—take care—the first time I took her liberty—the second—

GRANDIER

Oh! You wouldn't dare touch her life, I hope?

JEANNE

Why not?

GRANDIER

At that very moment, I will call and accuse you.

JEANNE

Who then has an interest that Ursula ceases to live? The one she can accuse, it seems to me. First of all, she is in my power. You don't know where she is. I am free and you are a prisoner—oh, you are silent! The demon is advising you, no doubt. Well, if you were to give me the supreme joy of choking me with your own hands, I who have nothing left to expect on earth where you disdain my love—oh! You would gain nothing Grandier—you would gain nothing for her—for I've foreseen everything before. I came down here, and the order is given to kill Ursula, if, at midnight, those who hold her prisoner have not seen me return. Now, do you still hope? Do you still threaten? Do you still wish to struggle? Make yourself at home—call Grandier, call!

GRANDIER

Jeanne, you are mistaken. I have a way of saving, Ursula.

JEANNE

You! You!

(She laughs.)

GRANDIER

You are forgetting what God said to the wrongdoer, "The evil you meditate will overwhelm you, and your violence will fall back on your own head?"

JEANNE

You are preaching, Urbain, you are preaching!

GRANDIER

You are forgetting what God said to the just, "I will arm your heart with a mysterious strength, I will arm your spirit with an unknown power? Those that you look on will pale with fear—those you touch will fall to the ground."

JEANNE

Great God!

GRANDIER

"Make war on evil," says the Lord, "strike them in their pouring out of scorn and anger with an extended hand, with an inflexible and all powerful arm."

JEANNE

(shouting)

Help me! Help me!

GRANDIER

Jeanne—sleep!

JEANNE

H'hhh-help—me!

(The jailor opening the door.)

JAILOR

Here I am, Madam—you called me?

GRANDIER

Send that man away.

JEANNE

No! No!

GRANDIER

I wish it!

JEANNE

(shutting the door)

Leave us!

GRANDIER

Where is Ursula?

JEANNE

I won't tell you.

GRANDIER

Say where Ursula is—I wish it.

JEANNE

(struggling)

Oh! Oh! Oh!

GRANDIER

Speak!

JEANNE

She is in the forest of the Island Bouchard, between the Chapel de Buis and the crossroads of Ormes.

GRANDIER

The assassins are waiting till midnight?

JEANNE

At the Rock of Saint Maure.

GRANDIER

Fine! Now in this cell, there is a secret door. Find it!

JEANNE

No, no, no.

GRANDIER

Find it and tell me where it is. I wish it!

JEANNE

(walking backwards)

Help me! Help me!

GRANDIER

The secret! The secret! The secret!

(Jeanne puts her finger on the black point in the middle of number 5 of two of the sculptures on the wall—the door opens)

GRANDIER

Oh! The door! The door!

(grabbing his sword, he says to Jeanne)

And now sit down and wait for me.

JEANNE

(gnashing her teeth)

Ah!

CURTAIN

ACT III

Scene 10

The Forest of the Isle of Bouchard. Snowing.

GRANDIER

(enters excitedly)

Here I am in the forest of the Isle of Bouchard, here I am at the Rock of Saint Maure—I crossed the forest without following the road. Never mind—here indeed is the cross roads of Ormes down there, and I passed near the chapel of Buis, it's really here she said they were waiting for her—it must almost be midnight. Eleven thirty sounded at Richelieu as I crossed the border of the forest. Oh, if she deceived me—or if she was herself deceived, if Ursula—while I am waiting here— Didn't I see something move down there in the midst of the trees? No, nothing. By good luck, this night is as clear as dawn. O, my God, thanks for these miracles you have performed in my favor! What is that noise? I was mistaken, it's the noise of some branch which bends and breaks under the weight of the snow— Oh—this time—no, it's the wind. If I call, if I call, Ursula, perhaps she will hear and will answer me—yes, but perhaps my cries will put her assassins on the alert. Silence! Oh, yes, silence! I really hear something—it's the crack of a whip. It's the noise of bells. Some coach is running post. It's coming from this side. Oh, if it were she they were carrying—we shall see!

(The postilion enters on horseback. A carriage with Barace and Maurizio.)

POSTILION

Oh! Oooh!

MAURIZIO

(from the windows)

What's wrong and why are you stopping?

POSTILION

Say, don't you see that down there?

MAURIZIO

What?

POSTILION

It looks like a man or rather like a ghost in the roadway.

MAURIZIO

Man or ghost—who cares! Keep going!

POSTILION

I told you, leaving the town, it seemed to me we were being followed.

MAURIZIO

If we're being followed, all the more reason to go quickly—forward, forward!

POSTILION

My horses are frightened.

MAURIZIO

You are frightened, wretch, and not your horses. Keep going or I'll blow your head off with a shot from my pistol.

POSTILION

All right, since you insist.

(starting up)

GRANDIER

Halt and get out!

POSTILION

Eh! Didn't I tell you so!

GRANDIER

Is there a woman in the carriage?

BIANCA

Yes, yes, yes.

MAURIZIO

(opening the carriage door)

Who are you? What do you want with me?

GRANDIER

I ask if there's a woman in that carriage?

BIANCA

Whoever you may be, help—help—they are taking me away in spite of myself. They are taking me by force. They are using violence on me.

GRANDIER

It's not her voice, but what does it matter! The oppressed always need help. God wouldn't have sent me on this road if he didn't want me to help her.

MAURIZIO

(sword in hand)

Who are you? What do you want? It's the second time I am asking you. Man or ghost reply.

GRANDIER

Maurizio dei Albizzio.

MAURIZIO

Urbain Grandier! I thought you were in prison, magician?

GRANDIER

No, no, I am free! Free to prevent evil plans—and—

MAURIZIO

Ah, Grandier—you are going to pay me once and for all.

BIANCA

Grandier! It's Grandier!

MAURIZIO

On guard!

GRANDIER

Lord Maurizio, it's not you I am angry with.

BIANCA

Grandier, my protector, my friend, you who have already saved me twice, don't abandon me—they are taking me away from my fiancé. Help me! Help me!

GRANDIER

Lord Maurizio, it's the will of God that those who love each other be united. Give this girl up to her spouse and pass on your way.

MAURIZIO

I already told you to put yourself on guard.

GRANDIER

Lord Maurizio, I am no longer a quarrelsome soldier, I am a poor monk, don't force me to use a weapon I had not taken up against you.

MAURIZIO

Ah, you were less humble than this in the Church of St. Peter, wretch! On guard—one last time, on guard!

(threatening him with his sword)

GRANDIER

Bianca! Before God, do you take me as your protector?

BIANCA

(falling on her knees)

Yes, Before God, yes!

GRANDIER

Then pray for this man; he's dead.

(Swords cross, Maurizio is wounded.)

BIANCA

Great God!

GRANDIER

Oh—now for Ursula.

BIANCA

Don't leave me.

(Midnight sounds in the distance.)

GRANDIER

Midnight.

URSULA

(in the distance)

Help! Help!

GRANDIER

The voice of Ursula, I am here, Ursula, I am here!

OLIVIER, BARACE and NOGARET

(in the distance)

Ah! Wretches ah, bandits! Death! Death!

(Clashing of swords—pistol shots.)

GRANDIER

Ursula!

(The gentlemen pursue three bandits who flee.)

URSULA

(entering)

Urbain! It's you—free, free when I thought you were a prisoner—Oh—miracle!

OLIVIER

(in the distance)

Wretches!

GRANDIER

Over here, Mr. de Sourdis, over here!

URSULA

He saved me, Urbain—some men were dragging me near this rock where they said someone was waiting for me—they were going to murder me—no doubt about it.

(noticing Bianca)

A woman!

GRANDIER

(to Olivier, who enters)

Mr. de Sourdis, while you were saving Ursula, I was saving Bianca—you see—we are quits.

OLIVIER

My friend—! Oh—whose body is that, Bianca?

BIANCA

Alas!

OLIVIER

Maurizio!

GRANDIER

God made me guilty, Mr. de Sourdis, so you should remain innocent—if you had killed the brother, you could not marry the sister.

OLIVIER

Grandier, my friend—what can I do for you?

GRANDIER

I confide Ursula to you, sir—let her be the friend of Bianca.

OLIVIER

Oh—her sister, mine, on my life, Grandier, on my life!

URSULA

But you, you, Urbain, what will become of you?

GRANDIER

Ursula, I have an account to render to God and man.

URSULA

Urbain! Urbain!

GRANDIER

Goodbye, Ursula, we shan't see each other again until in the above—and happy we'll be the first who goes to wait for the other.

(he leaves and in passing, throws his sword in the river)

OLIVIER

Come! Let's go!

BIANCA

(pointing to Maurizio)

That man was my brother, Olivier.

NOGARET

Oh! He's only wounded.

OLIVIER

Let's leave, let's go! He will take you back again.

(Exit Olivier and Bianca.)

BARACE

Here, he's coming to himself.

MAURIZIO

Ah!

NOGARET

Sir, dispose of us.

BARACE

We are at your orders, sir.

MAURIZIO

Then take me back to the town and try to get me there before I die.

NOGARET

Oh! Oh! You really have something pressing in town?

MAURIZIO

Yes, I have to avenge myself.

(They carry him to the carriage.)

BLACKOUT

ACT III

Scene 11

The Church of Saint Peter. The church has been converted into a tribunal. In the rear on a platform are the ecclesiastical judges—to the left is Grandier on a platform raised only two steps. In the back are the assistants.

MIGNON

Have Sister Louise des Anges, Sister Catherine of the Presentation, and Sister Elizabeth of the Cross retire. The sitting is suspended to give some rest to the exorcists.

BAILIFF

(aside)

The fact is they should be fatigued, after five hours of playing their comedy.

GRILLAU

(at the back)

Let me pass, let me pass—he's my child, I tell you.

GRANDIER

(to the Ecclesiastic Judges)

My brothers, you have reproached me for not accepting the confessor you wished to give me—I told you I was expecting one in whose piety and enlightenment I have total confidence. Here is the saintly man I was waiting for, my brothers, I beseech you to let him come to me.

CROWD

Yes, yes, that's just—you have the right to condemn him but you don't have the right to refuse him a Confessor.

MIGNON

That's fine, we grant him even that, we wish to be indulgent to the very end.

GRANDIER

(smiling)

Thank you, my brother.

GRILLAU

(embracing Grandier)

Grandier, my child!

(During this scene, each one leaves his place and talks, as is done when a hearing is in recess. Mignon is in the midst of a group, gesticulating. The monks and the other ecclesiastical judges seem to employ all their efforts to prove Grandier is guilty.)

VOICE

(in the crowd)

All the same, they don't want to confront him with the superior.

A SCHOLAR

Look, she isn't strong in Latin, sister Louise des Anges—she took quoties for quando.

ANOTHER

Yes, but as sister Catherine correctly said, "Adoro Jesus Christus," eh! It appears the devil has horror of the accusative.

ANOTHER

Not like Mignon.

(They laugh.)

GRANDIER

(to Grillau)

Oh—I knew for sure you would come.

GRILLAU

I received a letter from Daniel and I ran.

GRANDIER

Where is Daniel?

GRILLAU

I noticed him in the midst of a group of scholars—it seemed to me he had the air of leading a movement in your favor.

GRANDIER

Poor child! And my mother?

GRILLAU

I met her as I arrived, on the highway.

GRANDIER

What's she doing there?

GRILLAU

She's waiting for Mr. de Laubardemont.

GRANDIER

My mother, a holy woman like her, to ask something for me from that infamous man?

GRILLAU

Eh! My God—she's your mother, and for her son, she would pray to Satan.

GRANDIER

Yes, they warned me he was coming. Where was he then, that he arrived so quickly?

GRILLAU

He was in Tours and he's come to preside at your trial.

GRANDIER

Say, he's going to pronounce my sentence, father.

JEANNE

Oh! How can you say that?

GRANDIER

Perhaps, I am mistaken, so much the better for him.

GRILLAU

So much the better for him?

GRANDIER

They've made the monk suffer so much, that the soldier has returned. Let them beware! I will rule my spirit by his spirit and so far as he is just, I will be merciful.

GRILLAU

I don't understand you, Grandier.

GRANDIER

You know how sometimes I speak for myself alone and for God?

GRILLAU

And God also speaks to you, to you, my son, for your mother has told me everything, and God alone could have revealed Ursula's existence to you.

GRANDIER

Yes, to save her once, God spoke to me, but to save her a second time last night—Father, pray for your son—your son has blood on his hands.

(Noise in the crowd.)

GRILLAU

Huh? What are you saying then?

GRANDIER

Silence, Father! I believe something extraordinary is happening.

AN USHER

(announcing)

Lord Jacques de Laubardemont, Commissioner Extraordinary of His Majesty Louis XIII.

CROWD

Ah, that's him—that's Laubardemont, it's the King's judge. Yes, and the Cardinal's hangman.

USHER

Place for Lord de Laubardemont, place!

LAUBARDEMONT

Greetings, fathers. Hello, gentlemen. Usher read the commission from His Majesty so no one will be unaware of my authority.

CROWD

What a nice judge! He's the father of the Superior of the Convent of the Ursulines. Great! It's the daughter who accuses and the father who judges.

USHER

(at the foot of the dais)

Silence, gentlemen!

(reading)

"The Lord de Laubardemont, councilor to the King in his State Council, will go immediately to Loudon to investigate diligently

Grandier. On all the facts which have been charged previously against the above-mentioned accused, and others who may be newly discovered, concerning the possession of the Nuns of the Ursulines of Loudon and other persons who they say are also possessed and tormented by demons through the evil deed of the aforesaid Grandier—to institute and complete his trial without regard to any adjournment which may be demanded by him. In our palace of Amboise, this 5th of December, 1633, signed Louis."

LAUBARDEMONT

Where is the accused?

GRANDIER

Here I am, Milord.

(The two men look at each other.)

LAUBARDEMONT

Your full name?

GRANDIER

Urbain Grandier.

LAUBARDEMONT

Your age?

GRANDIER

Thirty-five.

LAUBARDEMONT

Your position?

GRANDIER

Superior of the Brothers of Mercy of Loudon.

LAUBARDEMONT

You are accused of having, by magic and witchcraft, and by virtue of a pact with the Demon of delivering to the Enemy of Mankind, the Mother Superior of the Convent of the Ursulines and several of her nuns.

GRANDIER

I am accused of this crime, it's true; but with the aid of God, I hope to triumph over this accusation.

LAUBARDEMONT

So be it, but for the moment at least, appearances are against you.

GRANDIER

Our Lord has said, "Don't believe in appearances."

LAUBARDEMONT

We are going to examine the facts.

GRANDIER

I am ready to refute them.

LAUBARDEMONT

Four pacts have been found with the nuns.

GRANDIER

I deny they were made by me or with my participation.

MIGNON

It is very easy to deny.

LAUBARDEMONT

Here they are clothed with your Signature and that of Satan.

GRANDIER

I don't know if the signature of Satan is real, but I know that my signature is false.

MIGNON

Then you accuse us of wishing to deceive, Milord?

GRANDIER

I accuse no one. I am afraid of being falsely accused.

LAUBARDEMONT

Now the nuns have recognized the pacts in virtue of which they were possessed.

GRANDIER

That is to say they have declared they recognize them.

MIGNON

Then they have lied?

GRANDIER

May God pardon them if it is with evil intent.

LAUBARDEMONT

How is it, if the nuns are not really possessed, how is it they are able to see at a distance and that one of them, Sister Louise des Anges, saw you from her cell, talking with the bailiff in the Hotel de Ville.

GRANDIER

What day did she see that?

LAUBARDEMONT

Day before yesterday, says the transcript.

MIGNON

She saw him as I see you.

GRANDIER

The day before yesterday?

MIGNON

Yes.

GRANDIER

Indeed, you say it was the day before yesterday?

MIGNON

Without a doubt.

GRANDIER

But the Bailiff is here—let him answer.

BAILIFF

I affirm, on honor, not to have seen Grandier the day before yesterday except in his cell; I affirm on honor not to have set foot in the Hotel de Ville for a week.

(Murmurs in the crowd.)

USHER

Silence, gentleman!

GRANDIER

Moreover, I repeat, the right of the accused, his first right, his most sacred right, is to be confronted with his accuser. My principal accuser is the Mother Superior of the Ursulines—I demand to be confronted with Jeanne de Laubardemont.

LAUBARDEMONT

That's all right—she will be made to face you in your prison.

GRANDIER

No way in my prison, for they can still falsify the report as they had falsified others.

(murmurs)

Not in my prison—here in this church, in presence of all men, in the face of God—and that, not tonight, and not tomorrow, but right now.

LAUBARDEMONT

That cannot be.

(Murmurs.)

GRANDIER

Why can't that be?

VOICES

Yes, yes, he's right. Confrontation. Confrontation. The Mother Superior. The Mother Superior.

LAUBARDEMONT

The Mother Superior is locked in her cell with two holy men who are praying God to deliver her from the demon that this man has put in her.

(Murmurs.)

GRANDIER

(to Grillau)

Father, something tells me that, if I call this woman, she will come despite herself.

GRILLAU

Call her then, call!

GRANDIER

Do you think that I have the right?

GRILLAU

Yes.

GRANDIER

That it may not be a sin to force the will of a human creature?

GRILLAU

If it is a sin, I take it on me. Call, call!

GRANDIER

Lord de Laubardemont, you refuse me, Urbain Grandier—accused of magic and witchcraft by the Mother Superior of the Ursulines of Loudon—to confront my accuser, Jeanne de Laubardemont?

LAUBARDEMONT

I refuse to disturb her prayers.

GRANDIER

Take care—I too, I can pray to God, and God will grant my prayers.

LAUBARDEMONT

And what will you demand of God?

GRANDIER

I will ask him to bring Jeanne de Laubardemont here, in spite of the two monks, who assist her, in spite of you, in spite of herself.

LAUBARDEMONT

Do it.

GRANDIER

One more time, you refuse.

LAUBARDEMONT

I refuse.

GRANDIER

In the name of the living God, who reads our hearts and judges our intentions, Jeanne de Laubardemont, I adjure you to leave your cell and to come renew the accusations you have made against me in my absence in front of me; God gives me the power to order you in his name. Come, Jeanne! Come, come, come!

(He remains with his arms extended; each turns and waits. Murmurs which announce Jeanne. Movement—they see her appear—she walks slowly, solemnly—noise among the assistants.)

JEANNE

Here I am!

LAUBARDEMONT

Why have you come?

JEANNE

A voice called me which I am forced to obey.

LAUBARDEMONT

It was that of this man.

JEANNE

You called me, Grandier?

GRANDIER

Yes.

JEANNE

What do you want from me?

GRANDIER

I want you to repeat to my face the charges you made behind my back.

JEANNE

Question me, father, and I will reply.

LAUBARDEMONT

Jeanne de Laubardemont, for how long have you known this man?

JEANNE

Since he became Superior of the Brothers of Mercy of Loudon.

LAUBARDEMONT

Had you ever seen him before meeting him in this town?

JEANNE

Never.

LAUBARDEMONT

Have you some feeling of love or hate against him?

JEANNE

None.

LAUBARDEMONT

Jeanne de Laubardemont, have you accused Urbain Grandier of having given a love potion to Ursula de Rovère, Countess de Sable?

JEANNE

Yes!

LAUBARDEMONT

Have you accused Urbain Grandier of having made her pass for dead and hiding her in his cell?

JEANNE

Yes!

LAUBARDEMONT

Have you accused Urbain Grandier of having, through his witchcraft of driving the Holy Spirit from the Convent and of having caused a demon to dwell there, so that the most saintly girls, forgetting their duties, pass their nights in balls and parties instead of passing them in penitence and in prayer?

JEANNE

Yes.

LAUBARDEMONT

Then you see—in presence or in absence she accuses—and the accusation is very precise, it seems to me.

GRANDIER

My turn to question her now.

LAUBARDEMONT

Your turn to question her, you say?

GRANDIER

Yes.

LAUBARDEMONT

Jeanne, I forbid you to reply.

JEANNE

Oh—don't worry, papa.

GRANDIER

With the aid of God, you will answer me now.

JEANNE

Me?

GRANDIER

Yes, you!

JEANNE

Ah, rather than reply.

(turning to flee)

GRANDIER

(raising his left arm)

Stop.

JEANNE

(struggling)

Ah! Ah! Ah!

GRANDIER

Listen, everybody! For this time, you are going to hear the truth.

MIGNON

You see indeed this man has an infernal power.

GRANDIER

You declared you've known me only for one year—how long have you really known me?

JEANNE

For ten years.

(Murmurs.)

GRANDIER

You said you saw me for the first time in Loudon, Jeanne—where did you really see me for the first time?

JEANNE

In Bordeaux.

(Murmurs.)

GRANDIER

You said you neither love me nor do you hate me. Do you hate me or do you love me?

JEANNE

I love you.

(Murmurs, murmurs, astonishment.)

LAUBARDEMONT

What are you saying, Jeanne? What are you saying?

GRANDIER

Oh, wait! We aren't at the end yet. You said I made Ursula de Sable, Countess de Rovère, take a love potion, who poured it?

JEANNE

I did!

(Murmurs.)

GRANDIER

You said I hid Ursula de Sable in my cell. Who kept Ursula de Sable prisoner in the "in-pace" of the Convent of the Ursulines?

JEANNE

I did.

GRANDIER

Where did I find you when I demanded the key to Ursula's prison from you?

JEANNE

In the midst of a feast that the nuns were giving in the cloisters of the Ursulines.

(Murmurs.)

GRANDIER

Did I know of this feast, of preceding feasts or those which followed them?

JEANNE

You were unaware of all of them.

GRANDIER

To employ that key, did I employ any form of magic or sacrilege?

JEANNE

None. You said to me, "In the name of the Lord God, give me that key," and I gave it to you.

GRANDIER

Why did you hold Ursula imprisoned?

JEANNE

Because she loved you and you loved her.

(Murmurs.)

GRANDIER

When did you decide to make her pass for dead?

JEANNE

After my voyage in Italy.

GRANDIER

What did you come to Italy to do?

JEANNE

I came to offer you my hand, a dowry of 300,000 pounds, and the rank of Captain.

GRANDIER

How did I reply to this offer?

JEANNE

You refused it.

GRANDIER

Why did I refuse it?

JEANNE

Because you no longer loved me!

(Commotion.)

GRANDIER

Jacques de Laubardemont, what you have just heard is the exact and holy truth. Give the order that I return pure and justified to my cell, and all will be forgotten as it ought to be between Christians.

LAUBARDEMONT

Let them take the accused back to his prison.

(Commotion.)

GRANDIER

Take care, Laubardemont! I offer you peace, and you choose war, I propose to forget, and you take vengeance.

LAUBARDEMONT

Guards, did you hear? Obey!

(Murmurs.)

GRANDIER

One moment! I still have some questions to put to this woman.

CROWD

Yes, yes, let him speak! Speak Grandier, speak—we will defend you, if necessary.

GRANDIER

Jeanne, you said I refused your hand, your 300,000 pounds, and the rank of captain because I no longer loved you. Now tell why I stopped loving you.

JEANNE

Why? Because—my God! My God! Because—

GRANDIER

Speak!

JEANNE

Because at Bordeaux, one night—a night you were hidden in the reeds by the river, you saw—

GRILLAU

(low)

Oh! My God! Could it be?

GRANDIER

What did I see? Speak!

JEANNE

Oh! Must I absolutely speak?

GRANDIER

Yes—absolutely, you must!

JEANNE

Because you saw a man leave my house.

GRANDIER

What was this man to you?

JEANNE

He was my lover.

(Commotion.)

GRANDIER

Does this man still live?

JEANNE

He's living.

GRANDIER

Has he been punished as he deserved to be?

JEANNE

He lives covered with honors and dignities.

GRANDIER

Where is this man?

JEANNE

He is here.

LAUBARDEMONT

Wretch!

GRANDIER

Name him!

JEANNE

Oh no, no, I won't name him. No, you cannot exact such a thing.

GRANDIER

So be it, don't name him, I consent, but point to him with your finger—I wish it!

JEANNE

(slowly rises her finger to point at Laubardemont)

There he is!

LAUBARDEMONT

Wretch!

CROWD

Her father! The Judge! Laubardemont!

GRANDIER

Now, Jeanne, wake up—remember all you have just said—and let the memory be your punishment.

JEANNE

(waking and looking around her)

My God! Ah!

(recalling what she has just said)

Infamy!

(she lowers her veil and flees)

CROWD

Go away, cursed woman, go away—incestuous one—go—sacrilegious one—go away.

LAUBARDEMONT

Help, guards, to me.

(Frightful commotion.)

GRILLAU

You heard her—he is innocent, innocent!

LAUBARDEMONT

He lied!

GRILLAU

Two years ago in confession he told me all that was just said—by my white hairs, he is innocent, I swear it to you.

LAUBARDEMONT

It was the demon who inspired her. Only a demon could force a girl to accuse her father.

GRILLAU

And I, poor priest, I tell you it is God who wanted the crime to be discovered and wanted innocence to be recognized.

ALL THE PEOPLE

He is innocent! He is innocent. No more, Judge, no more trial, no more prison. Freedom! Freedom!

(They force the guards.)

MME. GRANDIER

My son!

DANIEL

My brother.

GRANDIER

My friends.

LAUBARDEMONT

Oh—curse that man and all his family.

MAURIZIO

Wait, Laubardemont, wait, I am bringing you succor.

(The separate and see a wounded man brought in on a stretcher.)

GRANDIER

Maurizio.

MAURIZIO

Yes, it's me, Urbain; my turn to accuse you, and I accuse you.

CROWD

You accuse! You! You!

GRANDIER

Ah! I had forgotten him.

LAUBARDEMONT

Whoever you may be, you are welcome.

MME. GRANDIER

Who is this man?

GRANDIER

Oh, mother, mother!

MAURIZIO

(partially rising)

Yes, I accuse Urbain Grandier of magic, of sacrilege, of homicide.

LAUBARDEMONT

Speak! Speak!

CROWD

Of magic, of sacrilege, of homicide?

MAURIZIO

(on his feet)

Yes, I accuse Grandier of magic—for everyone knows that last night Grandier was shut up in the city prison—and he left this prison without the doors being opened, without the jailors having see him leave.

ALL

Oh! Oh!

MAURIZIO

Yes, I accuse Grandier of sacrilege, for despite the command of the Lord, he used the sword under the holy costume which proscribes the sword.

ALL

Oh!

MAURIZIO

Yes, I accuse Grandier of homicide, for he gave me my death blow, and if you doubt it—

(opening his doublet)

Look at the wound. Do you recognize it, murderer? Here, look, look, look!

(falling at Grandier's feet)

ALL

Oh!

GRILLAU

Why—answer him!

DANIEL

But say it isn't true, brother!

MME. GRANDIER

Give the lie to that man.

MAURIZIO

You don't give the lie to the dying and I am dying.

GRILLAU

Gentlemen, gentlemen, that man is lying like the others.

ALL

Yes, yes, he lies.

GRANDIER

That man speaks the truth. I give myself up to the justice of men—implore for me the mercy of God. I abandon myself to you.

LAUBARDEMONT

Take him back to his prison and this time set a watch on him.

CURTAIN

ACT IV

Scene 12

Grandier's prison—a grill in the rear across which a sentinel paces, musket on his shoulder. Grandier, Grillau, guards are present.

CLERK OF COURT

"We ecclesiastical judges, assembled under the presidency of Lord de Laubardemont, councilor on the Council of State, and privy councilor to the King, named extraordinary commissioner in this case have declared, and declare Urbain Grandier Father Superior of the Convent of the Brothers of Mercy of Loudon, attainted and convicted of the crime of magic, sorcery, and homicide, the first two on the persons of Ursuline nuns of Loudon and the last on the person of Count Maurizio dei Albizzio, in reparation for which we have condemned and do condemn the aforesaid Grandier—to make honorable penitence, bare headed, rope around his neck, before the principal gate of Saint Peter du Marche, and before that of Saint Ursula of this city and there, on his knees, to ask pardon of God—the King, and justice, and that done to be conducted to the Court of the City Hall to there be attached to a stake on a pyre which will be erected in the said place, and there to have his body burned rapidly, with the pacts and magical characters remaining attached.

Pronounced in one of the rooms of the prison of Loudon, to the aforesaid Grandier—the 6th of December, 1634." Have you heard?

GRANDIER

Yes.

CLERK

Will you sign the warrant as is the custom?

GRANDIER

In confessing to the crime of homicide, yes—but rejecting those of magic and witchcraft.

CLERK OF COURT

(presenting him a pen)

Do as you please.

GRANDIER

"I admit being guilty of homicide on the person of Count Maurizio dei Albizzio for which I indeed humbly request pardon by God, but I deny all the other crimes imputed to me by the aforesaid warrant. Grandier." There's what you wanted, sir.

CLERK

Have you any request to make?

GRANDIER

None, and I thank my judges for having spared me the torture.

(to Grillau)

I will see you again on the route with my mother?

GRILLAU

Neither of us will be missing at the last moment.

GRANDIER

As for Daniel?

GRILLAU

Well—?

GRANDIER

Try to get him away—he's a child and such a spectacle will kill him.

GRILLAU

Alas! We have not seen him since last night.

GRANDIER

Wherever he is, so be it. God is with him.

(Grillau leaves)

GRANDIER

(turning)

For what time, gentlemen?

CLERK OF COURT

For this morning, at nine.

GRANDIER

Thanks—go Father, go.

(He sit on a bench—The Clerk and Guards leave. The last one receives a purse from Daniel's hands as he slides behind the soldiers.)

DANIEL

Brother! Brother!

GRANDIER

Ah, it is you, Daniel.

DANIEL

Hush.

GRANDIER

How'd you get in?

(wrapping him in his cloak)

They told me they had forbidden my prison to mother and you.

DANIEL

I gave all I had to the guards and they seem not to see me—so I slid between them.

GRANDIER

Poor child, do you know what you are exposing yourself to?

DANIEL

Me?

GRANDIER

Didn't you hear that man shout a curse on me and all my family?

DANIEL

God will protect me and then, besides, it was necessary I see you at all costs—they are busy trying to save you, Grandier.

GRANDIER

Who is?

DANIEL

Mr. de Sourdis.

GRANDIER

You've seen him?

DANIEL

Yes.

GRANDIER

What has become of Ursula? What has become of Bianca? The only misfortune that can happen to me now is to be unaware of their fate and to die ignorant of it.

DANIEL

Bianca has already her bridal gown, she married Mr. de Sourdis last night. Ursula is already dressed as a novice; she enters the Carmelites tonight.

GRANDIER

Then they are all praying for me; I am at peace for the prayers of two angels will have preceded me to heaven.

DANIEL

Now brother, let's speak about you.

GRANDIER

About me?

DANIEL

Yes, on my way here, I crossed the court of the City Hall.

GRANDIER

Well?

DANIEL

In that court I saw a pyre.

GRANDIER

It's mine.

DANIEL

Oh—I passed by very quickly, but listen, it's not that danger that I suspect the most, because as I told you, Mr. de Sourdis is busy about saving you.

GRANDIER

And what other danger do I run?

DANIEL

Brother, Mr. de Laubardemont was at City Hall speaking with two soldiers—I saw him smile. I was suspicious of them. I followed these soldiers, I was a stranger to them. They paid no attention to me; I overheard what they said when they rejoined their comrades.

GRANDIER

And what did they say?

DANIEL

They said Mr. de Laubardemont was afraid of the scandal of a public punishment, they were speaking of the testimony of the Mother Superior which could be revived, they added that Mr. de Laubardemont would give even a 1,000 pounds if an accident befell the condemned.

GRANDIER

Yes, I understand.

DANIEL

Then one of the soldiers said, "An accident, by God, that's easy. The guard who guards Grandier walking before the cell bars, has only to lower his musket, as if to disarm it, the dog escapes and the bullet follows. That would be found to be an accident."

(While Daniel is talking the sentinel pushes his musket through the bars.)

DANIEL

Oh, brother, the man who said that—

(Daniel hurls himself in front of his brother. The shot is fired.)

GRANDIER

Ah! Who was that shot for?

DANIEL

For Daniel, happily—embrace me, brother—I am dying!

GRANDIER

And I thanked them for having spared me torture.

(Taking Daniel in his arms and putting him on the bench.)

OLIVIER

(entering)

What's wrong? And what was that shot?

SENTINEL

An accident, officer, in un-cocking my musket, as the wick was lit, it went off.

OLIVIER

It is I who command the escort which must escort the prisoner to the stake. Open for me.

(The jailor opens.)

OLIVIER

Grandier! Grandier! Ah, there he is—listen, Grandier—it's I who command the men who must escort you—these men are mine—in the corner of the place Saint Croix, ten horses are saddled and waiting, eight are ridden by cavaliers. The other two are for you and me—when we pass near those horses, we will jump into the saddle, in four hours, we will be in Poitiers. There ten other horses await us, tomorrow, we'll be at La Rochelle—in three days we'll be in Spain. Ah, indeed, it's the least I can do for you, for you who gave me Bianca. That is to say, my life, and who will die for having given her to me. Why, what's wrong? You don't answer—Grandier! Grandier!

GRANDIER

(weeping)

Look! Look!

OLIVIER

Daniel, killed—killed by that shot!

GRANDIER

You see clearly, I cannot escape, Mr. de Sourdis, for instead of one, I now have two deaths to expiate.

BLACKOUT

ACT IV

Scene 13

The court of the City Hall—to the right a façade with a balcony. Steps on the same side. Scaffolds at the rear—arcades through which one enters the court. In the center, the pyre, guarded by soldiers.

GRILLAU

And you will have the courage to wait for him here?

MME. GRANDIER

Didn't the Virgin follow her dying son to the foot of the cross? My name is Mary like her—and my son is innocent like hers.

WOMAN

Say, folks, you don't know, they say the nuns have retracted and that they made so much noise because they were amorous of him.

A MAN

(entering)

Oh! It's an infamy. It's an indignity.

WOMAN

What? What?

MAN

Misfortune will befall him.

WOMAN

To whom?

MAN

To the infamous Mignon.

WOMAN

What did he do now?

MAN

As Grandier finished making honorable penance at the gate of the Church of Saint Croix, Mignon gave him a gold crucifix to kiss.

WOMAN

Well? Well?

MAN

Grandier offered to kiss it, but hardly had his lips touched it than he screamed.

WOMAN

Bah!

MAN

"You see," said Mignon, "The demon is in him and cannot bear the presence of our lord."

WOMAN

Was it true?

MAN

Wait a while, then. Grandier called to Mr. de Sourdis with whom he spoke very low.

WOMAN

What did he say to him?

MAN

I don't know, but Mr. de Sourdis tore the crucifix from the hands of Mignon and plunged it into the holy water held by the sacristan—the holy water started to boil. The crucifix gave off fire and was burning like a red hot poker.

WOMAN

Infamy! Horror!

MME. GRANDIER

Thank God, with me, my sisters, his executioners are giving him an eternity of joy.

WOMAN

His mother! Oh—poor woman!

MME. GRANDIER

Is he still far off?

MAN

No—for here comes the executioner.

(Laubardemont crosses the stage amidst the murmurs of the

crowd—children who are on the scaffolding throw stones at him. He turns back.)

LAUBARDEMONT

Take care, burgers of Loudon! This stake erected for only one could really be used on several!

(He goes into the City Hall. New threats against him. His guards make a movement—the crowd recedes.)

SHOUTING

(from outside the courtyard)

There he is! There he is!

(Grandier, Olivier, guards and monks enter.)

WOMAN

(kneeling)

Holy Martyr, you will pray for me, won't you?

ANOTHER

Your hand, father, your hand.

ANOTHER

Let me cut a snip of your clothes—it's the dress of a saint.

GRANDIER

Alas, brothers, alas friends, I am only a poor sinner like you.

MME. GRANDIER

You see him—he's not a condemned man—he's a victor! Grandier!

GRANDIER

Mother.

MME. GRANDIER

Come my son, come, my Grandier, come!

GRANDIER

Oh—mother—mother!

MME. GRANDIER

I will be strong, fear nothing.

GRANDIER

Because you don't know all your misfortune, mother.

MME. GRANDIER

Grandier, I had a vision last night which changed my sorrow into joy; I saw you seated at God's right hand with a halo.

GRANDIER

Did you see me there alone, mother?

MME. GRANDIER

No, strangely, Daniel was with you and you both said to me, "Don't cry, saintly woman, we are both happy."

GRANDIER

Then, mother, God has told you what I dared not tell you.

MME. GRANDIER

Daniel must follow you?

GRANDIER

Daniel has preceded me.

MME. GRANDIER

He's dead?

GRANDIER

They killed him!

MME. GRANDIER

Two martyrs instead of one! My God, I am elevated above all mothers.

(The usher appears on the balcony, commotion in the crowd.)

USHER

(on the balcony)

Silence!

(reading)

"Warrant which condemns Urbain Grandier to the pain of death, as a magician, blasphemer, and murderer—

VOICES

(in the crowd)

Jeanne! Jeanne! The daughter of the judge—the Mother Superior of the Ursulines—barefoot—in the habit of a penitent.

JEANNE

(entering)

Yes, Jeanne, Jeanne barefoot, in the habit of a penitent.

CLERK OF COURT

(reading)

"We, ecclesiastical judges, assembled under the presidency of—"

JEANNE

Silence! Let me speak first and then you may read your warrant if you dare.

CROWD

Listen! Listen!

JEANNE

Yes, yes, listen everybody, and I wish the whole world was here to listen to me: This man is condemned but it is I who am guilty—this man is going to die—but it's I who deserve to die.

GRANDIER

My God, what's she saying?

MME. GRANDIER

It's written that nothing shall be wanting for your glory, O my son!

JEANNE

I loved you and it was that love which destroyed me—my hate was from love, my vengeance was from love, my impiety, my sacrilege, it was also from love. Oh—noble spirit, chaste heart, pure soul—

(falling to her knees)

Pardon me! Pardon me!

GRANDIER

Poor creature—wasn't it for a sinner like you that these words of

Christ were said—"Much will be forgiven you, for you have loved much."

GRILLAU

(making a sign for the executioner to wait)

My son!

GRANDIER

Yes—it's time, isn't it?

OLIVIER

(coming closer)

Grandier, say a word, make a sign—and you are saved.

GRANDIER

Monsieur de Sourdis, I commend Ursula to you.

MME. GRANDIER

(extending her arms to him)

My son!

JEANNE

(kissing the hem of his robe)

Grandier!

GRANDIER

Mother, be blessed!

(kissing the cross that Grillau presents to him, then mounting the pyre)

Jeanne, be pardoned!

(He holds out his arms, which they tie to the two branches of the stake.)

THE TWO WOMEN

Ah!

(The executioner sets fire to the pyre.)

CURTAIN

ABOUT FRANK J. MORLOCK

FRANK J. MORLOCK has written and translated many plays since retiring from the legal profession in 1992. His translations have also appeared on Project Gutenberg, the Alexandre Dumas Père web page, Literature in the Age of Napoléon, Infinite Artistries.com, and Munsey's (formerly Blackmask). In 2006 he received an award from the North American Jules Verne Society for his translations of Verne's plays. He lives and works in México.

www.ingramcontent.com/pod-product-compliance
Lightning Source LLC
LaVergne TN
LVHW041615070426
835507LV00008B/253